Raindrops
In the Dust

Dreams, Memories,
and Reflections

BOOKS BY EDWARD V. TUTTLE

Sacred Stories Sacred Dreams;
Bible Myth and Metaphor

Raindrops
In the Dust

Dreams, Memories,
And Reflections

Edward V. Tuttle

Pathways of Lights
Santa Maria, California

Publisher's Cataloging-in-Publication
(Provided by Quality Books, Inc.)

Tuttle, Edward V.
    Raindrops in the dust : dreams, memories, and
reflections / Edward V. Tuttle
      p. cm.
    Includes bibliographical references.
    LCCN 2003092338
    ISBN 0-9716484-0-9

    1. Tuttle, Edward V. 2. Authors, American--20th
century--Biography. 3. Clergy--United States--
Biography. 4. Spiritual biography--United States.
I. Title.

PS3619.U88R35 2003   818'.6
                QBI33-1558

To all the souls who have journeyed with me in this life, and especially to Linda Bearer Tuttle, without whose love, faith and persistence, this book might never have been born.

Acknowledgments

I wish to extend my sincere thanks and appreciation to a number of people for their generous support in bringing this project to a successful completion.

First, I thank my wife, Linda Lou, for her abiding love and faith in the value of the content of the work, and her insistence that it be produced in book form.

To friends, new and old, who have each added their special encouragement and support: Bill Alarid, mentor and friend, who once again walked with me through the various stages of the project; Lucia Capacchione, noted author and art therapist, who generously provided the foreword; Jonathan Young, Curator of the Joseph Campbell archives, who put his unique stamp on a review of the book; Joanne Blum, author and dear friend; and Michael Craft, psychotherapist and friend; each one taking time out of their busy lives to add their special touch to the book — and to my life.

Last but not least, my thanks to Perie Longo, poet and teacher, for her editorial guidance regarding the poetry pieces, and her enthusiastic response to the work as a whole, and to Gail Kearns, for her editorial guidance.

Foreword

Famous diarists throughout history have shown us the road to wisdom and self-discovery that resided within, inside their own lives lived fully. In the very act of writing her diaries, novelist Anais Nin discovered an essential part of her own unique unfolding as a woman, and as an artist, through her daily writing practice. Journal-keepers around the world have discovered the same truth over and over again: our most private moments and thoughts can lead us to a buried treasure of inner wisdom, to a gold mine of revelations and inner strength.

The writing path to higher awareness is calling people of all ages. For the past decade, there has been a growing trend toward memoir writing, journaling and autobiography. As a pioneer in journal therapy and writing as a spiritual practice, I have been delighted to see this movement mature, much the way a parent watches children grow up and come of age. People are capturing their dreams, experiences and feelings through the written word in record numbers. Alone and in groups, countless individuals are now tracking the intimate moments in their lives and sharing them with others.

This lovely book which you hold in your hands is a rare collection of such intimate moments. It is a testimony to the fact that the individual life deeply lived leads to the universal, to the heart of what it means to be human. Like Rainer Maria Rilke in his *Letter's to a Young Poet*, Edward Tuttle gives us the inside story: the agony and the ecstasy of the creative life. Mapping new territory in his psyche, he has shared a journey filled with crises, self-doubt, risk-taking and the inevitable chaos that is a necessary part of birth. He also shares his joy and delight.-

Although not written as a how-to book, this volume contains a wealth of ideas for readers who write — or desire to write. The sub-title alone — *Dreams, Memories, and Reflections* — could be a navigating tool for writing as a spiritual and creative practice. As you will see, these simple themes have yielded gems of insight and suggest possibilities for the reader's own self-explorations.

For example, how many dreams have you ignored because they seemed so silly? We often say, "I had the *weirdest* dream last night," and leave it at that. By contrast, Ed leaves no nocturnal stone unturned. His dream translations not only make fascinating reading, they illuminate and inspire us to try it ourselves. In their simplicity and elegance, these pieces invite us to read "the letters from the soul" that our dreams contain.

Tuttle's writing is as compelling as it is inspiring. I could not put the book down once I picked it up. But it is also the kind of book that wants to be revisited, chewed on and contemplated, in the tradition of Hugh Prather's *Notes to Myself* or Anne Morrow Lindbergh's *A Gift from the Sea.* In bite-size morsels of prose and poetry, the author leads us through the fascinating adventure of re-creating himself. At a stage in life when most people are retiring, Ed began anew. He writes about it from heart and soul, combining a child's playfulness with the wisdom of a sage.

As life expectancy lengthens, more and more people are living long past retirement age. This book can be a trusty companion for those who seek to begin anew. It offers inspiration for anyone seeking renewal or for those who choose to reinvent themselves at any age. For young people, *Raindrops in the Dust* is a treasury of insights from a man who has lived wisely and well.

Lucia Capacchione, Ph.D., AT.R.
Art Therapist and Author,
The Power of Your Other Hand and
The Creative Journal
Cambria, California

RAINDROPS IN THE DUST

Table of Contents

IV - Dreams; Letters from Within 109

V – Whimsy — Muses at Play 123

VI – Writing — Agony and Ecstasy 137

A Welcoming Word

What you are about to read is a collection of pieces written over the last fifteen years, one *Raindrop* at a time, and shared with a community of kindred spirits, friends and family. Publication in book form was given little thought, though some pieces have been published as individual articles and poetry. The experience of writing *Raindrops* has been, and continues to be, a journey into the inner reaches of my own being, while learning and polishing the craft of writing to fulfill a dream delayed.

The saga began in earnest in Columbus, Ohio, November 1987, when we cashed out everything we owned, packed a thirty-three foot motorhome, and headed west. We named our home on wheels *Merlin* and it carried us into a magical time of play and renewal, exploration and discovery.

With unfettered time on our hands and a leisurely pace, major decisions of the day related to when to go to the pool or, where to travel to next. We read books, drank wine, talked into the night, loved, laughed, and dreamed of what the future might hold.

Most days began with the question, "Did you dream?" Then sipping strong black coffee and munching on a piece of toast, we would share our nocturnal dreams and their meaning, as part of our daily mind-play, often with remarkable results.

The practice became a daily habit and dreams and their interpretation, their special offerings of wisdom and guidance, provided a number of *Raindrops* scattered throughout the book. One suggested the title and the manner in which I was to approach the work, (*Raindrops in the Dust* p. 107), while another painted images of the typical blocks and challenges that writers encounter, and pointed to their resolution, (*A Writer's Dream* p. 135).

Other writers traveled with us on our journey, whose books opened portals to previously unexplored regions of my being, and revealed a new landscape of creativity and undeveloped talent. They were: Julia Cameron's *The Artist's Way, A Spiritual Path to Higher Creativity*; *Drawing on the Right Side of the Brain, A Course in Enhancing Creativity and Artistic Confidence*, by Betty Edwards and, *The Power of the Other Hand; A Course in Channeling the Inner Wisdom of the Right Brain,* by Lucia Capacchione.

Encouraged by the offerings of these mentors I plunged below the surface of life as I had known it — lived it — to explore the hidden and unexpressed energies, talents, and dreams that lay in that veiled realm of the unlived life that resides in each of us.

Many of the pieces came from something called *"Morning Musings,"* an idea lifted from

Julia Cameron's book *The Artist's Way* that required a time set aside each morning for writing. Her assurance was that it didn't matter what emerged, the idea was simply to move the pen with no concern for the result. It worked magic in getting past the surface stuff of ego, and kept me returning again and again to the blank page.

Using *inner dialogue,* a practice outlined in *The Power of the Other Hand,* by Lucia Capacchione, put me in touch with parts of my inner life in ways that were surprising in their wisdom and their humor. I welcomed, invited, and embraced my Muse, and she graciously responded in O *Muse, Come* on page 43.

Socrates said that the unexamined life is not worth living, and the Talmud suggests that an unexamined dream is like an unopened letter. I found both statements to be utterly true. Was the process totally painless? No! But then neither is life.

Raindrops in the Dust is a sharing of intimate slices of one life, feelings and experiences, relationships and reflections that may awaken the reader to the rich humanity of his own life. And it is Life that we seek, bruising, brawling life filled with all its passion — serene and gentle life with its oasis of love and peace, and more — always more.

The search for just the right impulse, and the word to convey, it is as challenging as the work of the detective who seeks the solution to a crime. It is the chase, the movement from one clue to the next that is exhilarating and captivating. For the writer it is the chase from one word to the next and not just any word — it has to be the *right* word, and there is nothing to match the thrill of that capture.

That *feeling* is reflected in the following from THE SPEECH OF THE HIGH ONE. It captures perfectly both the chase and the reward.

Well being I won
And wisdom too
I grew and took joy in my growth
From a word to a word
I was led to a word
From a deed to another deed

The Poetic Edda
(ca. A.D. 1200)

I
Sight and Insight

How we see what we see when we look at the world around us, at our fellow man, our self and our God, determines the quality of our life every day — every moment of every day.

Bearing Gifts

They arrived singly, silently
Gathering in loose assembly

From the corners
Of mind
From the dark realm
Of shadow
From the deep
And mysterious regions
Of soul —
They gathered

Some playful —
Some serious — each with
Their own Thought
Their own Voice
To fill the blank page

Enduring
As carved stone
Fleeting
As the carefree days
Of childhood —
They gathered —

Raindrops in the dust

The Dawning

With sleep still trailing from my limbs, I walked the quiet morning hour among the familiar sights and smells of my home. An ordinary, everyday journey from bedroom to kitchen, a path trod thousands of times in search of steaming black coffee and some fruit or bread to break the fast.

Suddenly, in mid-stride, it was as though I was seeing it for the first time; the paintings, the books, the crumpled lap robe in Linda's favorite chair, the friendly homely clutter intensely alive in the light of the morning sun. In that moment my heart opened like a flower caressed by the morning sun, and my entire being thrilled to a deep and enveloping love and appreciation for this — our home.

We are so inclined to seek the new, the titillating, the lure and fascination of the yet-to-be, that we often miss the magic of the moment. It is true, as Joseph Campbell has written, it is like we stand on a street corner waiting for the light to change, totally unaware of the "sword in the stone" at our feet. The ordinary conceals the extraordinary, the familiar the mystery.

There are moments like these scattered throughout our days, our lives, when we awaken briefly from our habitual sleep-walking existence to be touched by the Divine.

Another occurred in the late afternoon in Big Tree Park, near Angel's Camp in northern California. We had just parked Merlin among those awesome sentinels that have graced our land since before the birth of Christ. One cannot be among those towering giants without feeling the Presence of the Divine — without being awakened to the spiritual sense that "He restoreth my soul."

Rays of the late afternoon sun pierced the towering tree tops to lay patches of gold on the soft brown earth, and on the lush green grass of a nearby meadow. The peace, the serenity and beauty, was palpable as I sat, a guest, in the sanctuary of God's cathedral.

Lines from God's World by Edna St. Vincent Millay came to mind.

> *Long have I known a glory in it all*
> *But never knew I this;*
> *Here such a passion is*
> *As stretcheth me apart —*
> *Lord, I do fear*
> *Thou'st made the world*
> *Too beautiful this year;*
> *My soul is all but out of me —*
> *Let fall no burning leaf;*
> *Prithee, let no bird call.*

Caught up in the fullness of it I sat sipping a glass of wine, when into the stillness there slipped the skirling of a lone bagpipe. I was transfixed. It was the masterful, completing touch of the Great Artist upon the scene, and upon my heart. I was utterly consumed by the magic of the moment, so choked with emotion I could barely breathe.

There is a growing sense of an awakening — a dawning — in the consciousness of the human family that is global in its sweep yet, like all such movements, very personal and individual in its happening. Often it takes the form of events like those above, that poets and lovers, minstrels and song-writers, and ordinary folk like you and me have briefly awakened to over the centuries.

They are not calculated to happen, these moments of grace — of joyful, blissful insight. They cannot be planned, for they do not appear on demand. Often they arrive in the night.

It was February 1971, and I lay in the intensive care unit at Los Robles Hospital in Thousand Oaks, California. While test-driving a new motorcycle I had hit a patch of loose gravel and slammed into a tree. The result was a fractured pelvis, compound fracture of my lower left leg, extensive internal injuries and a critical loss of blood. As I hovered between life and death I had a vision, one that changed my view of life forever.

The Vision

In the near distance I saw a massive stone building surrounded by an expanse of manicured lawn, dotted with ancient oak trees — a place of monastic tranquility. A dozen monks strolled about the grounds in pairs, conversing quietly. I moved as an unseen observer from one pair to another and listened to their talk, the pattern of which was always the same.

One would make a statement taking a position on an issue as a matter of absolute truth. The other would always initially agree saying, "Yes, that's true, but do you see?" And then would lead the dialogue step by gentle step, with irrefutable logic, to the exact opposite position as being equally true.

A flash of insight coursed through my body like an electric shock. Thrilled and excited to the core of my being, I exclaimed, *Wow! That's it!* The world of duality in which we commonly live, and move, and have our being, was in that instant replaced by the soul-shaping realization of a Sublime Wholeness. Nothing and no one was left out. There was only the One, the All-ness of God, and Life and — everything! fit!

I lay quiet, I don't know for how long, in an effort to hold the sense of it close and not have it slip away like a dream. The rapture of it filled my senses while the details faded; only the certainty of the awesome truth of the experience remained — etched into my soul forever.

I wish — Oh, how I wish — I could share with you one brief example of their wise and gentle dialogue, to share with you the feeling — the absolute certainty of the Truth of it — the Wholeness, the Completeness and Unity of all creation. But I cannot find words of sufficient strength or depth to carry the experience from my mind and heart to yours.

Experiences like these, brief glimpses of what Carl Jung called the Numinous, are the stuff of the spiritual revolution that is occurring, and is global in its reach. *"It is like leaven that a woman took and hid in three measures of flour, till it was all leavened."* (Luke 13:21). Like the dawning, it can be neither hurried nor impeded in its own majestic movement.

What might we do in order to be a conscious player in its movement? We might realize that these gifts of insight come when the objective mind — the "monkey" mind — is quiescent as in meditation, contemplation, or just day-dreaming, when we are, in a sense, caught unaware, open and receptive. It is then that we are most likely to see the extraordinary in the ordinary, the mystery in the familiar, and be open to the touch of the Divine.

Concerning the unforgettable vision of the monks and their dialogue, I would like to tell you that everyday of my life thereafter I acted out of a total awareness of that illumined moment. Alas! I cannot. But I have a strong sense that the same or a similar experience can be yours, and can come at the most unexpected moment. Perhaps the end of The Vision holds the key.

I was privy to the knowledge that the conversing monks were soon to part, to go their separate ways to different areas of the world as teachers.

Perhaps you have had the good fortune to meet one.

A team of talented doctors repaired the broken and torn parts of my body and I lay in intensive care for five days. During that time I had two more unforgettable experiences.

A Healing Presence

The first came in the night. The lights were dimmed, and the muted sounds of the hospital whispered their assurance that all was well. I lay awake listening to the comforting rhythmic beep of the heart monitor. I felt little pain, and that only when I tried to move, which was seldom. I was thankful to be alive, and content to let the quiet of the moment fill my senses.

As I lay there on my back, I was startled to feel two hands cradling my buttocks, and gently adjusting the area. The feeling lasted for several moments, several precious moments, while my heart filled to bursting with the wonder of it. I was alone in the room, yet obviously not alone. There was Someone present with the comforting, reassuring, and healing hands.

Synchronicity

The second remarkable thing happened on the third day when a major earthquake struck Northridge, in the San Fernando Valley, about twenty miles away. I heard the crash of glass, and a frightened scream. The hospital rocked and swayed as though shaken by some playful giant, while I wondered what floor I was on. After a few moments everything settled and the quiet routine of the hospital was again in place.

I picked up my Bible and it fell open to Psalm 118, one I had never read before, and I read these unforgettable words, (I have strung excerpts together for brevity).

The cords of death encompassed me
The snares of death confronted me.
In my distress I called upon the Lord.
To my God I cried for help.
From his temple he heard my voice,
My cry reached his ears.
Then the earth reeled and rocked,
The foundations of the mountains
Trembled and quaked.
He reached from on high ...
He brought me forth into a broad place.
He delivered me.
He girded me with strength
and made my way safe.

The words leaped off the page, the synchronicity was breathtaking. The earth had indeed reeled, rocked, and quaked, and I *was* being lifted and girded with strength and — my way made safe.

Soul Nourishment

Poetry is a song written in the heart, for the heart. It is the distilled essence of the mystical union of emotion and word; it feeds my soul. Nothing moves me more in mind and heart than a line of poetry. In an instant I am in a different space, the lines quickening memories and dreams — beckoning the spirit. I close my eyes and I hear the call —

I must go down to the seas again
To the lonely sea and the sky
And all I ask is a tall ship
And a star to steer her by
And the wheel's kick
And the wind's song
And the white sails shaking
And a gray mist on the seas face
And a gray dawn breaking

These lines from *Sea Fever*, by John Masefield, touched my young heart and fired my imagination long before I ever went to sea. The Sea — the word never fails to conjure up images mysterious, vast, unknown and unknowable; and yet with all that there is a sense of intimacy, like the pull from a dimly remembered home.

I have stood alone on the foredeck of a ship under sail at midnight with the deep and mysterious sea below, and the vast canopy of the heavens above, and felt both insignificant and yet somehow at one with the All of it.

I need only to close my eyes to feel the throb of the engines through the soles of my feet, the rhythmic rise and fall of the ships bow, the sharp fresh wind in my face, and the taste of the sea on my lips. In memory I can still hear the hiss and slap of the waves against the hull, all of it a symphony of the sight and sound, the magic and adventure of my hero's journey. I was invincible — then.

> *I must go down to the seas again*
> *To that vagrant gypsy life*
> *To the gull's way*
> *And the whale's way*
> *Where the wind's*
> *Like a whetted knife*
> *And all I ask is a merry yarn*
> *From a laughing fellow rover*
> *And a quiet sleep and a sweet dream*
> *When the long trick's over*
>   John Masefield
>   *Sea Fever*

Sight and Insight

Ralph Waldo Emerson wrote, "The skill to do comes from doing" and, "Do the thing and you will have the power." I had a dream that dramatized those two truths.

Words appeared before me sharp and clear, along with the understanding of how they are made even clearer and sharper by manipulating their size and spacing.

Then a flight of steps appeared before me. As I began to climb them the first step grew to such a height that I had to climb over it, as a small child might when first negotiating a stairway. I finally succeeded, then paused to examine the remaining steps.

As I focused on them, a power was unleashed from my mind that shrunk each step until it was only a few inches high. I climbed the remaining steps with ease.

The elegance and economy of image that our inner mind, that subconscious realm of our being, uses to convey its messages never ceases to amaze and delight me. The creativity and clarity of the symbolic language as it relates to our waking lives is truly astonishing.

The first paragraph relates to the primary activity that fills my days — writing — and suggests how the words can be made sharper and clearer by changing their size and space, their selection, and placement. What is portrayed is a formula for effective rewrite, a necessary activity in the production of any quality writing.

The flight of stairs leads up to a higher place, to a higher level of talent and result, all of which requires effort as in climbing.

When the first step increased in size and difficulty to the point where I had to struggle like a child to navigate it, it was symbolic of how hard that first step is in any new discipline. But the drama says take heart, have faith.

For though you struggled mightily to negotiate that first step, having done so, the others appear to shrink in size and difficulty making the rest of your climb to the top easy. And the power that was unleashed in the dream is the fruit of the successful struggle that took me to that first level.

There is an ancient wisdom saying:
What I hear, I forget. What I see, I remember. What I do, I understand.

It is in the doing that we grow in power.
If it were your dream you might see it with a completely different meaning, no less valid. Dreams are like that.

What Do YOU See?

I look but often
Do not see
I see often
But not with my eyes
With what do I look?
How do I see?
For long it was
Such a mystery

Now when I look
I more often see
Beyond the appearance
The Reality!
Seeing more clearly
I look to relate—
To examine, observe
Appreciate —

The beauty, the ugliness
The parts and the whole
The atom, the heavens
Man — and his soul

Looking, I see
And seeing, perceive
Understand at time
And at times believe
What I see to be true
The Truth Supreme!

36

But looking anew —
See but a dream
So sometimes I look
And see that's true
And sometimes I see
The same thing as you
But, sometimes I look
And still do not see

Do you ever suffer
The same fault as me?

Mind —
The Super Computer

We often hear the human mind compared to a computer and the analogy works — up to a point. Its limitations become obvious when we considers the vast array of activities that the mind is engaged in at any given moment, and the unknown potential yet to be discovered on our evolutionary path.

Emerson wrote, *"There is One Mind common to all men, and each is an outlet to it, and to all of it"* and, *"We lie in the lap of an Immense Intelligence which makes us receivers of Its Truth, and organs of Its Activity."*

Contemplating Emerson's words we might see that we are like individual computer terminals in a vast cosmic network of Mind — the InterMind — a microcosm of the Macrocosm. And since we are exact replicas of the One, made in its image and likeness, see that we are hard-wired for Wholeness, and recognize that as the Master Teacher proclaimed, *"The Father (the Wholeness), and I are one."*

Playing with the analogy, one can easily appreciate that we often misuse the mind much as we do our computers. That *"garbage in, garbage out,"* computerese for bad programming, applies as inevitably to our mind as it does the computer.

We might then realize that the software running in our computer, made up of the concepts, beliefs, and attitudes that we have gathered over the years, is the source of most of the problems that plague us. However, since *this* software is our own creation, or at least a product of our acceptance, it lies totally within our power to delete, modify, or simply to write new programming. The idea inspired —

My Computer

I have my own computer
Always close at hand
It listens to me carefully
That I might understand

It uses every word I speak
It chooses not its own
And so I reap the full results
Of every thought I've sown

My word, thought, and image
Is all it will record
And faithfully create my world
From each and every word

It operates so wondrously
So quick — it seems like magic
But when I fail to include love
The results can be quite tragic
My computer doesn't think at all

It just receives and acts
To give me what I've asked for
Choice is what it lacks

I sometimes do forget to see
My computer is always ON!
Accepting thoughts I do not want
Then things come out all wrong

My computer has tutorial
It teaches me the way
To use it more effectively
When working, or at play

It makes my life so easy
With talents so sublime
I'm grateful every day I live
My computer is ON-LINE

Wired with perfection
Connected to the Source
Potential is quite limitless
Except for me of course

I have my own computer
Now I am quite aware
Its primary instruction is —
HANDLE ME WITH CARE!

The Interrobang?!

My journals are liberally sprinkled with thoughts, ideas, and observations that end in an unusual display of punctuation in which a question mark is combined with an exclamation point — "?!". The combined marks provided a perfect symbol for a mind as un-made-up as a bachelor's bed, one that was open to every side of an issue — inside, outside, up-side-down, and inside-out. The life-changing awakening that I experienced in *The Vision* (p. 26) would not be satisfied with anything less.

With one exception I could no longer accept the idea of *absolutes,* God being the only exception. But man has contrived to create his own image of God and name it absolute, and we know the havoc that has created.

My use of the strange punctuation not only satisfied some inner urge, but worked as a symbol of the omnipresent paradoxical nature of life itself. Nothing is single in nature even God is dual within His/Her Wholeness, and the symbol presents the same universal statement as the Yin/Yang of Taoism, where one is constantly changing into the other. The question mark is Yin; feminine, open and receptive, while the exclamation point is clearly Yang; masculine, dominant, and unyielding.

Their interaction, like the Yin/Yang, is a constant flow into the other and back. In philosophic terms, consider the continual movement from thesis to antithesis, resolving into synthesis, which in turn becomes the latest thesis and it becomes clear why it is the perfect symbol of the open questioning mind.

Imagine then my surprise and delight when on a trip to Florida I walked into a funky, friendly, store in Cocoa, a town not unlike Carmel or Ojai in California, and found a book, by Norman C. Habel, with the symbol on the front cover! It had a name — *Interrobang!*

In the opening pages of Habel's book I learned that it was "the first new punctuation mark since 1671," and was the creation of Remington Rand, one of the people who produced that now ancient writing instrument — the typewriter. Habel opened his little book with the following.

Interrobang

What's that?
Well,
It's like me!
It's like life!

It's mystery
And madness
All in one!

It's like asking why
And saying yes
In the same breath!

It's like facing
This life
And wondering
About another!

It says soul
And sass
In one sign!

It means
A bunch of unanswered prayers
And unlimited shouts!

It says
Life is worship,
Worship is a party,
And we are invited
To interrobang
Without ceasing!

Interrobang! Bang!

II
Morning Musings

Welcoming the Muse, and embracing the inner artist, is an adventure in faith — a journey beneath the surface mind into the dark uncharted realm of the subconscious for hidden treasure.

O Muse, Come!

O Muse, come! Stir up the dust of my soul. Let your light and laughter, your darkness and tears, take shape under the movement of this pen. Let the fullness of Life breathe deeply here; crying, sighing, groaning with the ecstasy of Being.

Reveal only the tiniest of your treasures and it will be sufficient to lift this day, this life, to the heights of joy. Reveal thyself, if only a small portion, the smallest glimpse. Fulfill your divine purpose. It is safe. I await your sweet presence.

I am here, Oh solemn one. You to whom distance has been so important now seek intimacy? Let it be so. All I have ever sought, all that I ever need, is an honest, open and loving invitation. I am here!

So, now you want breakfast. Your mind wanders so easily from the request, the desire, of only a moment ago. Any distraction, any sanctuary no matter how empty that offers escape from the challenge, seems to suffice. Of what are you afraid?

Is it that you want me to do the work, present the gift on a platter, while you are but a happy observer? Alas! That I cannot do. Stir up the dust of your soul? Only you can do that.

47

For it to be otherwise would be to rob you of the very thing you seek, hunger for — to create out of the realm of your own soul, your own life. Only in that is the authentic revealed. It is sufficient.

Ah! You want to be perfect, is that it? "Produce but do not possess," is too great a leap, though you wish it were not. Set out to create the worst, the dullest, the most disappointing of children. Though it seems the result is not what you desire, it is the doing, the process that is important.

It is that which will stir up the dust of your soul to reveal the treasures, if any, that exist there. It is the movement, the doing, the journey that you seek. The Act!

Creative energy is unleashed in the act, the energy that fashions universes, and the tiniest of creatures. It is the joy of doing the thing that IS the thing, and reveals itself AS the thing. This you already know.

Do not refuse yourself any longer. Move past the fear, the unknown and unrecognized blocks. Claim it! Risk it! It is not for the world, it is for you, and I am here for you!

Ah! You don't know what to write, what to paint? That's good! Pick up the pen and move it! Pick up the brush and — move it! The movement, the moment, will reveal itself. All you need is to trust enough just to show up, and to do it!

I am here!

Worry Not!

My back is tired, my butt is sore
I cannot read this anymore
My mind so filled with theories and stuff
My weary spirit cries — enough!
I must get up, and wash my face
And thus return to the human race
To live this day, and do it well
And worry not of Heaven or Hell
The essence of wisdom this must be
And surely the Truth
That sets me free

Man or Butterfly?

There is a marvelous story told by the Chinese mystic Chuang Tzu of his dreaming that he was a butterfly. His dream was so vivid, so real, that he felt the thrust of his wings carry him on the soft breezes from flower to flower. It was as though he danced on the wind, was one with it. He was thrilled with the feeling — so alive!

The experience was so real that when he awoke he wondered — *Am I a man dreaming I am a butterfly, or a butterfly dreaming I am a man?* The following dream reminded me of the story.

I am on stage speaking to a group of people. Behind me there is an array of plants and flowers, and as I speak they move forward to surround me, merge with me, until only my face remains visible. I have become a giant sunflower with my face in the center of the blossom.

A Dream within a Dream

I am a seed fallen into
The soft earth
Embraced
The earth breaches
The hard, thick shell
I have grown
Eagerly now
I push through
Into the Light
Ah! How glorious!
Life surges in me
Roots reach deep
Earth's juices fill me
While above —
I grow straight and tall
Sun moves and I with it
It disappears!
I am again in the dark
But, no! It isn't dark
The Moon —
And countless stars
Fill the night
I wait and watch
Then — a Light!
The Sun drinks
The morning dew
From my face
Born of the Sun
I am —
The Sun's flower

A New Day

The morning breaks
And I with it
Petals unfurling
Toward the sun
My heart
An open wound
My mind
Mute, illiterate
My Soul
Two hands
Reaching up

The Awakening

Slowly, reluctantly, I awake
Bound hand and foot
Confusion fills my mind
Fear grips my heart
A silent scream
Of hopelessness
Terror clogs my throat
As I struggle
To free myself

Who has done this to me?
While I slept!
Who could have done this?
I examine the shackles
Reflected In each
A greedy mouth
Lusting eyes
Grasping, clutching hands
Behind every image
A face
An all-too-familiar face

Circles

He drew a circle that shut me out
Heretic, rebel, a thing to flout
But Love and I had the will to win
We drew a circle that took him in!
Edwin Markham

The circle is the most naturally formed figure in all creation and is the oldest symbol for God — that which IS, without beginning or end — AM THAT I AM.   All movement in creation is circular and cyclical, everything bends back upon itself from the atom to the galaxies — to time itself.

Circles and Cycles

We begin as a circle
An egg in the womb
And circles on circles
We grow

On swift spinning earth
With it's cycle of days
And circling seasons
That flow

Day's golden orb
Night's pale, cool sphere
Set our world
Aglow

Circles and cycles
God's infinite plan
Reflected in all
We know

Cool ripe cherries
A round, red mouth
One's head
A ball with a brain

Spinning globe
Planet's path
Atom's form
A drop of falling rain

We begin as a circle
And as circles we grow
While death seems to wait
At the end

The journey complete
Think it not, my friend
We simply begin
Once again

Creative Play

At one of our church retreats we were each given a sheet of paper on which was drawn an empty circle, and supplied with a variety of coloring tools. We were asked to create a personal mandala. I created two.

One was a whirling vortex of color with red/yellow at the core and dark blue at the circumference, with a gradient of colors creating a spectrum in between. Outside the circle there were wispy clouds of color.

When we were done we were to contemplate our handiwork to see what our intuitive response might be. Following is the result.

I Am Life!

Primal whirling vortex
At the center — I Am!
The Sacred Fire
Eternal Flame
Within me
The Invisible One
Out of the One
Flows the many

Irrepressible
Irresistible
Infinite in form
And purpose

Burning hot
At the core
Cool and serene
At the edge
My whirling dance
Spins forth
Clouds of Being
I Am Life!

The other contained the Yin/Yang symbol of Taoism at the center, surrounded by pairs of symbols from astrology; Sagittarius/Gemini, Mars/Venus, Jupiter/Saturn.

Tao at Play

Everywhere you look
You see opposites;
Black/white
Male/female

A game you play
While looking at
Two halves
Of a Whole
Two ends
Of the same stick
Opposite poles
One axis

You insist
They are separate
Impossible!
You insist
On splitting them
In half
And naming it
Reality!

What a funny game!

A Mouthful of Sound

The title comes from a recent dream, in which a man who could take a random mouthful of sounds and make sense of them, communicate effectively, even eloquently. I was intrigued by the idea. A mouthful of sound comes from a head full of sounds, a world full of sounds, a veritable cacophony of sound.

What an exceptional talent for one to have, the ability to take a series of grunts, groans, moans, screeches, scratches, soft and hard, mellow and irritating, and spacing them with intervals of silence communicate with another creature.

This wonder of wonders God has given many of his creations, but nowhere does it appear more developed, more infinite in its variety, than in man. For man uses it not just to communicate in the sterile sense of conveying information, but to connect with another in a special joining of mind, heart, and soul. How beautiful!

How wondrous it is, how magical, to be able to fashion a mouthful of sound into a song, or poem, that captures and echoes the pulse and rhythms of life itself in its glorious variety. Sounds that carry feeling on their backs, in their hands, that leap like lightening across empty space from mind to mind. Listen!

How Do I Love Thee?

How do I love thee?
Let me count the ways,
I love thee to the depth
and breadth and height
My soul can reach,
When feeling out of sight
For the ends of Being
and ideal Grace.
I love thee to the level of
every day's most quiet need,
by sun and candle-light.
I love thee freely,
as men strive for Right;
I love thee purely,
as they turn from Praise.
I love thee with the passion
put to use in my old griefs,
and with my childhood's faith.
I love thee with
a love I seemed to lose
With my lost saints —
I love thee with the breath,
Smiles, tears, of all my life!
And if God choose,
I shall but love thee better
even after death.

Elizabeth Barrett Browning

Such a mouthful of sound conjures up images, like a master magician's trick — sounds that have the power to leap across centuries, stir the heart with longing, and fire the imagination. In an instant we are transported.

Or like this from The Chambered Nautilus by Oliver Wendell Holmes.

Build thee more stately mansions,
O my soul,
As the swift seasons roll!
Leave thy low-vaulted past!
Let each new temple,
nobler than the last,
Shut thee from heaven
with a dome more vast,
'Till thou at length are free,
Leaving thine outgrown shell
By life's unresting sea!

A mouthful of sound can build a mansion, create a dream, fashion a vision, loose a whirlwind, or bring peace and serenity. It can embrace and uplift, or exclude and scorn. It can instruct or confuse, make clear or obscure, inspire or crush. What awesome power there is in a mouthful of sound.

Silent Sentinels

I was stunned — speechless! A great sadness gripped my heart. They had cut down my trees, my beautiful, graceful towering trees. Cut them down and dismembered them, leaving only the weeping stumps. They had stood in stately column along the western edge of the Allan Hancock College campus, like silent sentinels.

They were not really my trees and yet they were, with that special ownership that is found only in the heart. From the very first their hoary, towering presence had touched me deeply in some strange way. I felt an affinity with them. Each time I drove past them they seemed to call to me, to something deep within that I recognized only dimly. Scripture speaks of *"deep calling unto deep,"* and they seemed to speak to me as though we were kindred spirits.

I yearned to capture the essence of them with brush or pen; their strength, their beauty, their changing moods in sunlight and shadow. I failed. But who would not? Only the hand of God can create that. I longed to absorb their strength, to be held in the embrace of their enduring serene dignity. Their very presence nourished my soul.

When I saw them lying there in pieces, their raw stumps mute reminders that their roots still reached deep into the earth, I felt like I was witnessing the slaughter of friends.

I was seized by the same sense of loss, the same soul-wrenching sadness that filled my heart on the bloody beaches of the South Pacific so long ago, beaches strewn with the broken lifeless bodies of comrades. And the same unanswered question rose to my lips, *"Why?"*

Here living things of beauty and strength it had taken decades to grow, gone in a single day leaving only bare patches of turned earth where they had stood, earthen mounds reminiscent of freshly filled graves.

We all too easily, mindlessly, destroy that which we neither appreciate nor understand. We are so very good at destroying, and so very poor at honoring and preserving the life all around us. We have eyes, but do not see, and ears, but do not hear. It's the voice of the intellect disconnected from the wisdom of the heart that we hear, and heed.

We move on convinced that we are the vanguard of the righteous. The trees disappear, and with them the birds and the small creatures whose life is interwoven with the trees. And another piece of the world's soul goes with them, and — a piece of ours as well.

Celestial Timpani

It rained during the night but the morning is clear, with the sun brighter than ever. But, as I write, there is a steady hypnotic dripping of water somewhere near that is insistent in its beat — insistent, deliberate, and unvarying.

Now it's inside my head, my body. It's heard and felt in every cell, like the steady beat of a cosmic clock. Oh! It missed a beat! It did, and now it has stopped completely. Apparently it was some small pool of rain collected, some run-off moved by gravity, by the pressure and flow of the universe. But what else was it?

There! There it is again! This time a single drop, a pause, then three, another pause and then two, as though now that it has my attention it seeks to impart a message — but what?

Intermittent now, it speaks only as it gathers more of itself then — releases — plop! Soon it will stop altogether unless the clouds yield more of themselves.

Stopped now, it leaves a void. It could have easily have gone unnoticed. In its ceasing the entire universe has changed ever so little and — I with it.

The Oracle Speaks

Some years ago I was part of a gestalt therapy group that met in Santa Barbara. One evening the therapist suggested that we meditate briefly and while doing so to imagine that we are in the presence of the Oracle of Delphi. Once there, we were to ask the Oracle a question and wait for an answer.

I entered into silence and, after a few moments, found myself walking up a cobblestone street toward the Temple at Delphi. I entered and stood in presence of the Oracle, then realized that had not thought of a question, and none came readily to mind. I stood silently before the Oracle for some time, when to my amazement a voice shouted loudly in my ear — "RELAX!"

I came out of the meditation laughing, for without my asking the Oracle had spoken the very truth I most needed to hear.

Relax!

Relax! Relax!
My poor body cries
You drive me much too hard
Life by the inch is easy
Why move me by the yard?

What's the rush?
Why this mad pace?
Will the goal simply disappear?
Why not tomorrow
Or a month from now
Why not wait 'til next year?
You drive me hard
Rarely let me rest
You know I can rebel
I'll just quit, refuse to move
Make your life a Hell
What are these "A's"
You desire too much?
Life isn't lived by degrees
Let's practice some Zen
Use a lighter touch
Fill our days with more ease
Relax! Relax!
Move with the flow
Treasure and taste the now
Quiet your mind simply let go
Be like water —
Welcome the Tao.

There is a shrub that grows outside my bedroom window that I greet most mornings as I breathe deeply of the fresh morning air. We bless each other as we exchange gifts of life, carbon-dioxide for oxygen. It reminds me once again how connected we are to everything and — how dependent.

A Mutual Arising

The green shrub
Out side my window
I do not know its name
Yet we are one
Its sweet new buds
Stretch heavenward
Toward the Sun
Echo the yearning
That rises from my heart
From the soul of me
With the rising Sun
We greet each other
A mutual arising
Its essence sweetens
The soft morning breeze
I am filled, nourished
I breathe upon it
We exchange gifts of life
And love — the green shrub
Out side my window
Whose name I do not know

Tower of Babble

I have a stack of books on my night table that keeps growing weekly — daily. Some I have read well into, with others I have just brushed the surface. I call it my "tower of babble," but it is not the only pile of books to have grown around me. I find a clear space to lay one aside and it becomes rooted, establishes a base upon which others come to rest, and by some natural law of attraction a new stack is born. They populate my bedroom, my office, the kitchen and dining room tables with a veritable smorgasbord of information — of mental delicacies. I nibble here and there, sample this, taste that, and rarely do I complete the course.

Tower of babble is an apt description for it is not without its confusion. Like a child with too many toys I play with one, drop it and pick up another, only to drop that, and so on. Which one will capture my attention next to offer up its special secret, show me the path my soul is to travel?

Is the tower a useful meaningful presence in my life, or a fleeting titillation of the senses signifying little of value other than a ready source of distraction? Is it a help or a hindrance in my journey through life, my quest for meaning and purpose? Perhaps like the biblical version it is my reach for God. Conscious or unconscious there is the ever-present urge to discover the key, to unlock the ultimate mystery of life, to answer the questions, who am I, and why am I here?

I sometimes see the tower as more of an impediment than a help, and feel the urge to purge my life of these strangers, friends, and companions. Entertaining though they may be, they stand in the way, blocking my view of my Self.

This is my personal tower of babble, but the world itself becomes more and more the same with a colossal tower of babble, a cosmic ocean of books, ideas, advice and information — the World Wide Web. Can one use the web without being caught up in it?

Like the stack of books at my bedside, multiplied exponentially, it rises quite literally into the heavens. Like my very own tower of babble there is cause to wonder — is it a blessing or a curse? More likely it is a mixture of both. The jury is still out.

A Thin Place

I don't recall where I was or what I was doing when I first heard the phrase — a thin place. It seemed to whisper in my ear this is where you find God. Intrigued, I let my mind play with the image as a metaphor, with the question — where do we find it — this thin place?

The question echoed a note from my editor, "Needs a visual image ... describe it physically, if possible." How does one describe the indescribable? The eye cannot see it, not with the most powerful instruments of science. Only the heart can see it.

And yet like the wind, which one cannot see, there is evidence of its presence all around us: in the pause between the beat-beat of our hearts; between the ebb and flow of the ocean waters, and the quiet space between the exhalation and inhalation of our breath. It is the pregnant pause present within the rhythm of all life.

And more, it is the spaceless space between heaven and earth, between the visible and invisible. It is that borderless space where the human and the Divine meet, merge, and are one. It is a birthing place.

This thin place is God's workshop. All creation flows forth from it; stars, galaxies, sperm and egg are all born here. Infinite possibilities lie in this space waiting to be embraced, waiting for the breath of life to be breathed into their ephemeral form.

It is here, in this thin place, that man was "made in the image and likeness of God," born of Spirit. Made to dwell in both worlds, this God-man forgets his birthplace and wanders the world over yearning for home. When will he learn that what he seeks is right where he is?

Treasure Chest

Before my eyelids lift
In my hands
Is placed
A precious gift
A treasure chest
Remove the cover
And the gifts
Spill lavishly
Upon the surface
Of mind
Resting in the lap
Of mind
All the promise
And possibilities of —
This new day

Into the Silence

Close your eyes
What do you see?
The in-side of me
Cloaked in darkness
Breathless dark
Waiting for the light
Quiet, motionless space
Between breaths
Easy, gentle
Softly paced
Expectant
Patient listening
Ancient rhythm
Old as time itself
Older!
Womb of life
Quiet
Rhythmic
Beat
Of the heart

Ah-h-h-h-h!

My Body, My Friend

My body, my friend
Walking tree
Roots in earth
Branches in clouds
Faithful servant

Pleasure palace
Spirit cocoon
Temple of God.
Renews, replaces
Cell by silent cell

Life reaches out
Tastes, smells
Touches, holds
And releases
All in wondrous flow

Twins

Constantly we seek
The pleasures of life
As a desert-bound traveler
Yearns for water
Seeking, ever seeking
Higher highs
Greater gains
More joyous joys
While we know
Within the deepest
Reaches of our being
Hidden within the pleasure
Lurking there
Like an assassin
In the shadows
Is its twin — pain
Lovers grasp
Clutch, clench
Fleet moments
Of joyous joining
Hand, heart and soul
Flee the specter
Of dying passion
Parting, death
How quickly the sharp
Sweet pain
Of love's ecstasy
Disappears, dissolves
Not in the living

Vital pain of parting
But the empty chalice of
Indifference
But wisdom cries out
Risk the pain
Hidden in the joy
Accept the joy
Hidden in the pain
Know these two
Are not two
But one!

Peace and Quiet

A seductive lethargy envelops me in a soft woolen blanket. I pull it close about me with the silent promise, just fifteen minutes more before I get up and face the day. Suddenly the silence is shattered when outside my window, like some insane tortured insect, there is the wail of a brush trimmer sinking its jagged teeth into the unsuspecting shrubs and bushes.

Ah! It begins to recede as it seeks fresh victims elsewhere in our cluster of townhomes. A blessed silence returns, broken only by the intermittent huffing of the furnace as it responds to the early morning chill.

Oh God! The gnawing, tearing, gnashing insect is replaced by one that howls madly as it blows the residue left by the first off sidewalks and driveways.

Now it too falls silent, exhausted in its efforts and the furnace ceases its huffing and puffing. At last there is quiet.

But no, arising out of the quiet is the beating of my own heart, the sibilant sounds of my own breath, all of which we accept as silence in our noisy world. Finally, with these, my mind finds an easy peace.

We live in a universe of sounds until at last we are wrapped in that final mantle of quiet and laid to rest. We close our eyes for just an instant it seems, and when we awake we find that it is not we who have been laid to rest, it is merely that which served as our body.

Now at last there is blessed silence. But wait — what is that — that blinding white light, louder than any sound? And now, growing in the background are voices, many voices — choirs of angels!

God, are we to have no peace?

III
Relationships

"At the end of your life you will never regret not having passed one more test, not winning one more verdict, or not closing one more deal. You will regret time not spent with a spouse, a friend, a child, or a parent."

Barbara Bush

Genealogy of the Soul

Who am I?
Where did I come from?
Who are they
Those who went before?
My family tree?
But — there is
A genealogy
That echoes from
The depths of me
It's mother's milk
To my ears —
The laughing melodic
Voice of Ireland
The soft b-r-r-r-r
Of the Scot
And the pipes —
The haunting wail
Of the bagpipe
Resonates
Deep within —
Stamped in my genes
Its siren song
A rushing torrent
In my heart
Blood of my blood
Spirit of my spirit
This genealogy of
The soul

A Good Wife

On reflection, I realize now that I have had three good wives; the wife of my youth; the wife of my middle and maturing years who gave me a son; and the wife, the woman who now shares my bed, and the remaining years of my life. I remember too the other women, loving and generous of heart, who have touched my life with their gifts. Each one nourished this soul on its path. But none more than —

Linda Lou

She, my other half
Awesome combination
Love wrapped in leather
Large, capable, healing
Nurturing, hands
Who is this creature?
Known to me
Yet mysterious
Strong, yet
Easily hurt?
I am reminded of
Updike's woman —
Twenty years since I wed
Warm woman, white-thighed —
Wooed and wed — Wife
A good wife who can find?
I can — and did!

Our Children

The Persian poet, Kahlil Gibran, saw truly when he wrote of children in his beautiful work, The Prophet.

Your children are not your children.
They are the sons and daughters of
Life's longing for itself.
They come through you
But not from you, and
Though they are with you
Yet they belong not to you.
You may give them your love
But not your thoughts
For they have their own thoughts.
You are the bows
From which your children
As living arrows are sent forth

In the early morning hours of May 30, 1968, I awaited the arrival of my first born — my son. This living arrow would pierce my heart and open a portal I thought was destined to remain closed forever. I had resigned myself to a life without children of my own. My heart filled with a joy I could not have imagined as I hurried to greet him.

First Born

Precious new life!
As you make your way
Into the world — Welcome!
Soon the answer
Son or daughter
It matters not precious one
You are you!
Before we meet, I love you.
Precious new life
Welcome!
Your first cry echoes down
The corridors of time
A sound old —
But everlastingly new
I run to greet you
Precious new life
Love, light — welcome!
My eyes search
A man child!
My firstborn — my son!
Strong, and lusty
Perfect. Beautiful!
We kiss, my love and I
Words uttered from
A heart overflowing
Words never enough
Poor shadows only
Of the thing itself
Our hearts are joined

Our souls blend and merge
And at the center
Of our oneness
This blessed moment
This new life — our son
I leave
No longer the same
The night —
Cleaner, sweeter
Thin shimmering sliver
Hung in the night sky
New moon new life
And God saw all that
He had made and
It was good —
It was very good

My Son—My Son

Of all the bonds of love in my life, there is none stronger than that which binds my heart to that of my son. I have always had a strong sense of knowing and loving him before this lifetime. Perhaps over many lifetimes our souls have journeyed together in joy, and in pain.

My poem, First Born, speaks of his birth and of the immediate and awesome impact it had on my life, on my very soul. The years have swiftly — all too swiftly — slipped by, and now he is a grown man; a tall, handsome, intelligent, sensitive young man — abundantly blessed. But our journey together has held some painful rites of passage for each of us.

I doubt that any parent can look back over the growing years of their children and not feel the pain of regret at not being wiser in their love, their guidance, their being there for them. It was at such a time that my son expressed his pain in words that sunk deep within my soul — *"You Never Smile at me Anymore."*

The words lay like a lake of molten lava in my gut, a mad mix of anger, frustration, sadness and love — and would not let me be. Seeking relief, I dredged them up from the depths and laid them bare in following poem.

You Never Smile at Me Anymore

The words
Searing teardrops
My heart
A bowl of sadness
Gathered every one
His eyes
The eyes of my father
Clouded with hurt
Seek an opening
In the angry
Impassive face
I show
Their silent plea
Why can't you love me
As I am
As you once did?
My mute response
Love you! Love you?
It's because
I love you
I'm angry, and
Don't know
What to say
Or do
Through clenched teeth
He says
You won't give me
The money?
Resolve

Begins to crumble
It's hard to refuse him
Anything
Son, it's not the money
I can't, I won't
Be a part of your
Self-destruction
He leaves
His words
A brand
On my heart
You never smile at me
Anymore

Blue is the Color

Blue is the color
The primary one
The eyes of my father
The eyes of my son

Blue is for loyalty
Tried and true
For night skies and day
Though of different hue

One vast, dark and deep
The other, bright and gay
Indigo night
Soft azure day

Blue is for mood
Heart-breaking tale
Mournful soul notes
Lowdown "blues" wail

Sad melting sound
Pluck strings of the heart
Haunting sweet ballad
Lovers drifting apart

Blue is the field
Where stars are sown
In the proud waving flag
Of our home

Blue is the color
The primary one
The eyes of my father
The eyes of my son

Forgiven?

Dreams are written in the same language as myth, and like myth they often portray universal themes of guidance, encouragement, and healing. This dream dealt with a deep regret that I carried in my heart, one where it was too late for me to make amends. I felt it offered forgiveness from beyond the grave.

I am arranging two coffins. They are my father's and my mother's. They are not at all like coffins, but consist of an open framework over which a cloth is draped. I know that if I stack them, one on top of the other, I will not be able to secure them with one cover.

As I considered this, they changed into two regular coffins, both white and identical in every way.

All this took place on the country road in front of the house where I was born, and grew up. I keep pushing them further and further off the roadway, a little at a time, to the side of the road.

It had rained and the road was wet, and slick with mud. Little puddles of water dotted the surface. I succeed in moving the coffins far enough off the shoulder to be out of the way of any traffic. My final act was to arrange them precisely, and perfectly aligned, end-to-end.

I became aware of a presence behind me. Without turning to look I know it is a man sitting on the grassy bank in front of our old homestead. It is my father, and he is chuckling, as though he finds my efforts amusing.

The dream was clearly about my unresolved sadness and regret that I had not been present for either my father or my mother in their dying. The pain of my failure to be there for them, and for me, I had buried — had not wanted to look at.

The opening scene dramatizes how I really feel about the results of my failure to be there for them. Their bodies lie in open wooden crates left by the side of the road, improperly cared for ... unattended. The rain, collected in puddles, an image of tears unshed.

The initial open framework that served as their coffins suggested that there had been no closure. In my unconscious, it was an issue that was incomplete, unfinished.

The change into identical coffins underlined the fact that I was absent at the death of each. Both coffins were white, a color usually reserved for a child — pure and innocent. Could this mean that they, through my dream, blessed me with that which I could no longer ask of them — their forgiveness?

My great care in placing them precisely end-to-end was another sign of closure — putting an end to it. May fathers presence on the grassy bank, and my sense that he found my efforts humorous, were like a message from him saying, "What a lot of fuss; how funny!"

This too would have been very much in character. It was like a father watching a little boy with toy building blocks, very seriously engaged in making his world — just right.

Life Support

It is likely that my father and mother have each forgiven me for not being at their side at the time of their dying, but I still find it difficult to forgive myself. My father was at her bedside when my mother died, but who was with him when he drew his last breath?

I can think of nothing so devastatingly lonely as to die alone in the cold, sterile, alien confines of a hospital room, with life support tubes and monitors for company. That this was my father's experience is an especially painful memory that I live with, and will carry to my own grave..

Time of Death- 0400

Inert white mound
Trailing plastic veins
Red — yellow — clear
Vacant orbs staring
Watchful watch recording
Beep ... beep ... beep
Colored heads drooping
Plastic gut hanging
Drip ... drip ... drip
Frail fingers clawing
Silent cry keening —
I don't want — to die
Alone

Beep ... beep ... b-e-e-e-e-e-p!

A Choice for Life

He had not yet reached his first birthday when I carried him into the clinic and laid him gently on the examining table. The examination was brief and thorough.

"He's very ill," the doctor said. "He has hepatitis, a virulent form. I'm afraid we are too late."

My heart sank within me; he was so young and beautiful and — vulnerable. Tears welled up in my eyes, I asked, "What can we do?"

"There's nothing I can do here that you can't do at home," he said, as he handed me a bottle of pills. "These may help. Make sure that you give him one in the morning and another at night until they are all gone, and pray that it works."

I looked at him lying motionless on the table his soft brown eyes fixed on me, filled with utter trust. Mine were wet with tears. I picked him up and carried him to the car and laid him beside me on the front seat. He had not uttered a single whimper during the whole time.

When we arrived home my wife was waiting at the door. "It's not good," I said, answering the question in her eyes.

"He has hepatitis, and the doctor said there is little hope. He gave me some medicine for him, and suggested that we pray." I carried him into the house and placed him gently on a bed of blankets we had made for him in our small kitchen. His name was Laddie, and he was a beautiful tri-color border collie.

Morning and evening of the days that followed I would open Laddie's mouth and place the pill as far back on his tongue as I could, and then hold his muzzle shut until I was sure that he had swallowed it. The doctor had told me that he was to be fed nothing but cooked ground beef and rice. The menu got Laddie's attention and he managed to eat a little from time to time, but the days passed with no visible change in his condition.

It became my routine to carry him outside to place him on the grass to do his business. One day, after a number of long days of watching, and waiting, for what seemed to be the inevitable, I carried him outside. I put him down on the grass where he stood on trembling legs.

Indian summer was upon us blessing the world with its exquisite mixture of warm Sun, and brisk autumn wind. A stiff breeze buffeted and carried a colorful array of radiant fallen leaves over the landscape.

Laddie managed somehow to maintain his balance on legs weakened by the illness, his nose pointed into the wind. As I watched, he lifted his head and sniffed the air and, I saw something I hadn't seen for days — he wagged his tail.

In that moment I knew with a blazing clarity that he had *chosen* to live. And live he did for more than seventeen years — eating ground beef and rice every day of his long life.

It was some years later, when the image of Laddie sniffing the wind, wagging his tail, and deciding to live, filled my senses again.

I lay in the hospital following a motorcycle accident, my body broken, my life hanging in the balance. A nurse stood beside my bed holding a basin of hot water and a washcloth.

"Would you like me to wipe your face?" She asked. I nodded, yes. I watched her as she placed the basin on the tray table, and dropped the washcloth in the hot water. She wrung the excess water from it and laid it gently on my face, from my hairline to my chin. I reached up and held her hands and the warm wet cloth against my face.

The warm wet caress of it filled me with an intense joy, a deep and abiding appreciation of life and its wondrous gifts of love and, like Laddie, I chose to live. And every day since, each time I place a hot washcloth upon my face I remember that moment, and am filled to overflowing with the sheer joy and wonder of just being alive.

Sweet Torment

She wore a simple cotton shift that revealed nothing of the soft mounds and valleys that lay beneath, yet promised a delicious world of delight. It reached to just above her knees and, as she moved with sensuous grace, revealed flashes of white thigh. Desire stirred in me fueled by my imagination.

The room, the presence of others and their conversations, the social sounds of the gathering all faded into the background. I wanted nothing so much as to touch and caress, to separate those luscious thighs, to lay hold of the treasure hidden within.

It's no secret that a man's dreaming is often not confined to his hours of sleep. Perhaps it would be better if it was but that's not likely in the healthy male, or in the healthy female I would guess.

The evening ended and the vision quickly faded, with enough left over for a bit of poetry.

Hidden Treasure

A simple cotton shift
Over soft mounds and valleys
Promised a world of delights
Sensuous grace in motion
A flash of thigh, and
I was lost! Lost —
In a dream ... a fantasy
Of touching, caressing
Separating, revealing
The treasure
Hidden within

Forbidden Fruit

Her laugh —
Her music-filled laugh
Running up and down
The corridors of my mind
Stirs old memories
From the shadows of my Soul
Over the years — a lifetime —
Filled with love
Marriage, work, a son
Often unbidden
Wisps of memory
Like a subtle fragrance
Carried on the breeze
Flirt with my mind
And, for a moment
It all returns —
The love, the longing
The pain, the misery
The loss, the betrayal —
She was my best friend's wife

Wise Counsel

"In the night also my heart instructs me."
Psalm 16.7

I find portions of dreams remembered — dream fragments — to be powerful in their brevity, and the simple clarity of their message. Here are two examples that occurred on the same night, together with the messages as they appeared to me. Dreams, or dream fragments, on any single night are likely to have a common theme, although the connection is not always readily apparent. Here are the dreams.

Two women, my wives, own all the water on the island, specifically the rights to all the underground water on the island. Their names are Faith and Prudence.

I walk with care and dignity on a grassy field, reminiscent of a parade ground. I am fully clothed in formal attire, as one might be who occupies a position of importance, when on parade before the public. There is a line of spectators to my left, and an unseen, unidentified presence on my right. I walk with care, looking neither left nor right.

In dream interpretation it often helps to title the dramas. I named the first, *The Twin Virtues*, and the second, *Walk the Straight and Narrow*.

102

The thematic connection took shape as I related both dream fragments to the prior afternoon when I was given a massage. Surrendering to the luxury of the moment, I wondered what it would be like if I were to bed my masseuse.

It was a vision which in reality had no prospect of ever happening, but that has never stopped the mind from its play. In that light, the following is how I saw the message of the dreams.

I might wonder, but my unconscious is clear about the issue. My wife owns all the rights to the underground water (semen) on the island (I land). Faith and Prudence are the virtues to be practiced. My behavior, like Caesar's wife, is to be beyond reproach. *Faith* and *Prudence* are two qualities to which I must be wedded.

The relationship is to be a formal one, for in the second dream I am dressed in formal attire, coat and tails with a hat to match.

I walk with dignity before the world with the spectators (the public) on my left and an unseen Presence, (my Soul, my Conscience, the Lord of my Being), on my right. I walk a straight and narrow path between them, looking neither left nor right.

The dreams leave no doubt as to their message. There is a clarity of vision, wisdom and truth, present in our dreams that we do well to look for, and to heed — gifts of love and guidance.

Heaven-sent

Long ago and far away
There was a wondrous event
A child was born to common folk
Some said was Heaven-sent
Angels sang, shepherds watched
Gifts the Wise Men brought
They saw a star in the eastern sky
And seeing it, they thought —
We'll go and see what this portends
This star — so still and bright
And traveling down to Bethlehem town
They came on the strangest sight
In a place where cattle were kept
They found, a new born babe, a boy
Seeing the child, and the light round about
Their hearts were filled with great joy
For there in a manger lay the Son of Man
Reflecting God's infinite love
The eternal promise of peace on earth
They'd looked for, from heaven above
But, it's in the heart of man to be found —
This peace — this blessed event
And it's born anew
With the birth of each child
For each is —
Heaven-sent

The World You See

When the world you see around you
Is filled with gloom and doom
And you question the worth of living
While loneliness fills the room
You feel you have run the gauntlet
While the prize has faded from sight
And there's no one, you think—
Simply no one—
And nothing to set things right
Remember, my beloved
In the depths of your misery
To turn and look within you
To find Me in the world you see
For I am the Power within you
The Life, the Love, the Light
Greater than any condition
That appears in your darkest night
Greater than any circumstance
From which you seek to flee
I will free you, and lift you —
And light your way —
Out of your misery
When you turn and look
Within you
And find Me
In the world you see

An Unholy Union

Soon after I awake
I strap time to my wrist
Each day begins with this
Ritual, this union
For time and I are wedded

Only a moment ago
I was free
We part each night
Time and me
Yet, each morning

I offer my arm
To the shackle
Like the huge elephant
Taught from early life
That resistance

Is futile —
I submit — I submit!
To yet another day
Locked in
This unholy union

Divorce is impossible
Long as my heart beats
Its faithful rhythm
Marking
The passing moments

I will manage time
I vow
It will be my servant
Not my master
And time
Smiles

I am the master
I declare
Of my fate
Captain of my soul
And time
Chuckles

Oh, what the Hell!
I say
I'll strap the bloody thing
On again and ignore it
And time
Laughs uproariously

Home at Last

These words I uttered with a grateful sigh upon returning home from a two-week visit with family and friends in the east. I love them and do not see them often enough, but I was glad to be home. It was not an unusual reaction, and with good reason, for we are blessed with a beautiful, spacious home on California's central coast, a place that others only dream of visiting.

There is an old Indian saying that the heart seeks that place where one's name is *"written on the wind."* That is how I feel about California in general, and the central coast in particular.

So you can see, perhaps feel, some of the joy and comfort that I felt at being back home. But it wasn't until late that evening that my body joined in the celebration, when once again I lay in my own bed.

Down I lay my body weary
In familiar fold and dent
'Neath my head a friendly pillow
Home at last! I sleep — content.

IV
Dreams —
Letters from Within

The Talmud, Judaism's ancient book of law and wisdom, suggests that an unexamined dream is like an unopened letter.

Sprinkled within the pages of this book you will see that our dreams can offer forgiveness, wisdom, love, guidance, encouragement, and much more. A look at your own dreams will offer all the proof you will ever need.

Raindrops in the Dust

Gifts of wisdom, power, and beauty fill our dreams — sleeping and waking. They come wrapped in gossamer, fragile elusive wisps of image and symbol. For example, it was a dream that was the source of inspiration for this book, giving it shape and purpose, even suggesting the title. It also pointed to the way in which the work was to be done, one that would eliminate a common mental/emotional block that is likely to raise its ugly head at the beginning of any creative effort. Will people like it? Will it be good enough? Will it — I — receive their approval? Here is the dream.

I am alone in a small enclosed structure, plain and unadorned, shack-like in appearance. There are no windows and no decorations on the walls, which are plain wood. The floor is earthen.

Alone in the privacy of the place I find I am sexually aroused. The exquisite tension grows and peaks and the seed of life spills forth to splash randomly upon the earth like rain.

I hear an accusing voice say, "He left his seed in three places," and I am shown three sheets of paper, each marked with random patterns of small circles that represent the impressions of the spilled seed. The impressions remind me of those created by a spattering of raindrops in the dust.

111

I am asked to acknowledge that the impressions are mine, my creations. I proceed to write my initials in every one of them, but after doing so I have the uneasy feeling that I have ruined them. Had I simply initialed each page at the bottom, as one would a formal written statement, it would have been sufficient and would have left the impressions clear and pristine.

I shared the dream with my wife, Linda, and the words, *Raindrops in the Dust,* rang like a mantra in my mind. It struck me not only as an apt image of that which had taken place in the dream, but as a wonderful Zen-like description of the creative process itself.

In the symbolic union of life-giving Water (Spirit) and Dust (Earth) the process of creation is begun. I felt I had received a gift — and a mission. The imagery grew in my mind as a call to do that which I had talked about endlessly it seems — to write — to create.

All dreams, and dream fragments, are messages from the inner regions of mind and heart and, as the Talmud suggests, are like unopened letters. Taking a closer look at this dream, this is what I saw.

I was alone, engaged in a solitary act that is a substitute release of the primal energy that seeks expression in the act of creation. It is the particular energy that finds sublime release in the creative arts.

I stand upon the earth; I am *grounded* and, I am *discovered*. After I have acknowledged that the results are indeed mine, I am uneasy about the way in which I did it, initialing each and every impression.

I wondered what that meant, what it might suggest about the creative work, and how it was to be done. As I thought about this, Christ's statement that he was "*in the world, but not of it,*" came to mind. I have learned, when engaged in dream analysis, to pursue such a thought even though one might wonder what it has to do with the dream at hand.

What was he suggesting, this remarkable man who was clearly in the world, and of it, as we all are. What, then, did he mean, and how might it play into my understanding of the dream?

His statement pointed to a state of consciousness that allowed him to be fully engaged without being trapped in or swallowed up by the world and its concerns. Lao Tzu, revered Chinese philosopher and reputed author of the classic Tao Te Ching, pointed to the same attitude in the following:

They (Evolved Individuals)
Produce but do not possess,
Act without expectation,
Succeed without taking credit.
Tao Te Ching (1)

This was the key! The creative impulse is embraced and given joyous birth when the creative activity is devoid of any expectations. Being and doing — the care-less scattering of one's seed — **is** the Way.

Dust devils dance
As the wind whispers
Its promise
To the parched earth

A stiffening breeze
Heralds the approach
Darkened clouds
Brood on the horizon

Filled to bursting
Like a young
Mother's breast
They yearn for release

Ah-h-h-h!
Raindrops in the dust
So definite
So fleeting

A Song in the Night

I awoke in the middle of the night with the remnants of a dream swirling around me, and several lines of a song — words and melody — running through my mind. I laughed out loud as I replayed the words in my mind, and realized they were in the form of an incomplete song.

I turned on the light and wrote down the words, but the song lacked a bridge and a resolution. I let my mind play with the words and the thrust of the song's message, and happily I received both, and the song was complete.

The impetus and sentiment of the song never fails to bring a chuckle to my heart and a smile to my lips, even though they relate to a time of personal pain and loss.

I was in the midst of a separation from my wife, and a pending divorce. It was a time filled with a sense of loss, of confusion, of feeling adrift. Add to that the fact that I was a minister of the Science of Mind, drenched in positive thinking — master of my fate and captain of my soul — and you begin to see the dark, quirky humor of the gift from my unconscious.

Here are the lyrics.

I've Decided!

I've decided I'm not here
Today
I've decided I am
Far away
Somewhere far beyond
The stratosphere
One thing's certain
I'm not here — today!
I've decided I'm not me
Today
I've decided I will flee
Today
Flee and be a creature
Wild and free
One's thing's certain
I'm not me —
Today!
Now, deciding is important
For one who would succeed
A focused, fired
Inspired mind is all
You really need
But
My life has been chaotic
And my plans have gone astray
So, I've decided
Yes, I have
That I'm not here —
Today!

Yet, in the midst of all of that there was something strange and wonderful taking shape somewhere in the depths of me, for during the same period I had the following dream which I titled —

A Fish Story

I was kneeling next to a pool of water, part of a beautiful rock-fountain arrangement. Several large fat Koi fish swam in the pool. I reached into the water and picked one up. As it lay cradled in my hand it spoke to me in a soft, child-like, feminine voice.

"Oh, don't hurt me." It said.

I replied, just as softly, "I'm not going to hurt you."

The fish responded, "You are Brahmin." I gently placed the fish back into the water.

In my waking life I had never felt less like a Brahmin, a priest or wise one, a member of the highest Hindu caste, but I found the dream comforting, reassuring. Was my unconscious pointing to another reality, a dimension of my own being with which I was not yet in touch? Sometime later I purchased a house, and in the front yard there was a pool identical to the one in my dream. It contained a number of large, fat, beautiful — Koi.

A Garment for Mind and Soul

The interpretation of one's dreams cannot help but lead to the conclusion that our dreaming mind uses a language rich in imagery in a way that is masterful in conveying its meaning and intent. Our challenge is to play with the images intuitively to see how they might relate to our waking life. Consider the following dream.

The elevator doors opened and a man stepped forth and gave me a luxurious deep green, soft woolen outer garment. It was unique in shape and pattern with a wrap-around look, a flowing collar and a large hood.

I said, "Oh, I've loved this coat since the first time I saw you wearing it. It was the very first time I saw you."

I take the coat wondering if it will fit. I am concerned the sleeves may be too short. The gift-giver was of medium height, inches shorter than me. I have a little difficulty getting the coat over the shoulders of the business suit I'm wearing, but I finally succeed. The coat fits perfectly. I am delighted with the gift.

When I awoke, I let the dream play across my mind alert for its meaning. Its message began to take shape. I had just begun to teach a class in which I compared the mind/body disciplines of the Science of Mind and Taoism. I had for some years been strongly attracted to Taoism, and had tried to apply its principles in my life.

You might say that I had, from time to time, *worn it like a garment,* not always confident that it would *fit.* For many years I studied and taught the principles of the Science of Mind, a discipline in many ways the opposite of Taoism.

Though each is based on the acceptance of a Universal Order or Law (the way things work), the manner in which they respond to that Law is diametrically opposed. The Science of Mind seeks to direct the Law, while Taoism seeks to observe the Law in action and respond by moving with it. By conforming to its impulse and shape, one may influence its direction.

Much as the garment did when I put it on in the dream. It *conformed to make an easy fit,* even over a business suit. My strong attraction to Taoism was echoed in the dream, when I said that I had *loved it from the very first time I saw it.*

The message of the dream was clear. My unconscious was confirming my deep attraction to Taoism and its principles. Like the garment in the dream, it is *soft and flowing and is of unusual design.*

Taoism's most prominent symbol is water, a substance that easily assumes any shape into which it flows, which makes it a perfect metaphor for Taoism's basic principles of: nonresistance and noninterference. Over the years, I have come to appreciate that it, Taoism, represents the Yin energy needed to balance the strong Yang of the Science of Mind in my life.

My concern that the garment might not fit readily over the shoulders of a business suit proved to be unfounded. It does fit, and as a matter of business practice can be a very powerful, if unusual, discipline to apply in the business world.

I have grown very happy with the fit, and am delighted with the confirmation of the truth presented by the elegant symbolic language of my dream.

Dreams —
Sleeping and Waking

Here is a dream that triggered a childhood memory.

I stand looking down the length of an open area that is similar to a golf course fairway, with trees bordering both sides. It is autumn and the trees are dressed in glorious shades of gold and orange and red, with just a touch of the green remaining.

I take off my hat and put it aside, along with a walking stick I carry, and I begin to run. I run swiftly, silently, up on my toes, my feet hardly touching the ground. Overhead is the open vault of the sky. I feel a solitary joy in the freedom and power of my fleet movement over the ground.

The dream reminded me of a time when as a boy of ten or eleven I would run through the woods to my favorite fishing spot on Deer Lake. In my imagination I was not a young boy, I was a famous frontier scout running through Indian infested country where swiftness and silence was required for survival. As in the dream, I would run so lightly and swiftly that my feet hardly touched the ground.

Swift and powerful I ran, under my feet a carpet of golden leaves and overhead the pale autumn sun peeked through a canopy of bare branches, to which the remaining leaves cling defiantly.   These silent friends applauded my passage. What joy!

How much of our living is wrapped in fantasy? More than we think. People speak of *"walking meditation,"* or of running and *"being in the zone."* The feeling is one of being out of this world where time and space lose their usual significance — slip out of sight.

It happens for me when I lose my self in the chase for words to fit an idea, or when I am totally absorbed in capturing the line of a subject I want to sketch or paint. I experienced it yet again last night — in the dream.

Swift as a young stag
Silent as a bird in flight
His feet kiss the ground
Lightly, disturbing nothing
In his fleet passing
Autumn gold at his feet
A magic carpet
Lifts him on his way
Trees, alight with fire
Cheer his passing
And the stones —
Even the stones —
Join the chorus
Of silent exaltation
That thunders
In his blood

V
Whimsy —
Muses at Play

There is never a time when I do not have a number of projects and tasks pressing for my attention. But responding to the mundane daily inner litany of "you must," and "you should," wearies my soul.

My soul cried out for something fresh and unscripted, even unrecognized, that sought a voice, and so I resolved to spend at least an hour each day in play with the Muses — and play they did.

Twain's Truth

It was Mark Twain who said, "Whiskey is for drinking; water is for fighting over." Every few years, here in California, Twain's pithy comment takes on a new measure of truth, when periodic drought conditions reduce the water levels in lakes and reservoirs enough to cause a general concern.

The first season that brings heavy snowfall to our mountains, along with some seasonal rainfall to the parched land serves to quiet the rancor and the fear — until the next drought. But there always is a another one and when that occurs one hears the voices of contending forces and factions fulfilling Mark Twain's humorous observation. It inspired the following.

Water, Water, Everywhere

Water, water, everywhere
Or so we seem to think
Water, water, everywhere
But, is it fit to drink?

Casmalia spawns its wicked brew
While drought and fires shrink
The level of our reservoirs
Then deeper wells we sink

"Let's save our precious water"
Some sweet, faint voice does plead
"Without it life will perish"
But few there are who heed

Lawns must all be watered
Cars kept nice and clean
Streets and steps must all be hosed
Our golf course lush and green

"The neighbors, they must ration theirs"
Faint voice again does cry
We'll form committees to study it
Comes back the swift reply

Study groups proliferate
Agencies contend
Special interests join debate
Discussions without end

Environmentalists now are heard
The pocket mouse is in danger
That pipeline surely will disturb
Its cozy little manger

The weeks and months and dry years pass
Situation unimproved
While politicos sit on their —
Refusing to be moved

"Growth and progress, they're the key
There's water enough," they say
"Let's build that marvelous lifestyle
They have down in L.A."

The water, now a trickle
Drips in the kitchen sink
The air is rich in flavor
What is that awful stink?

The smell of growth and progress
We've moved up the scale a notch
Would you like a glass of water?
No thanks. I'd rather have a Scotch

Small Stuff

Some of the most ordinary occurrences can, if we allow them to, fill our days with frustration. And if we get caught in the warp, the vortex of our own negative emotional response, we can succeed in escalating the most trivial happening to a crisis of monumental proportions.

But, if we choose, we can look at the same situation with a sense of detachment, even amusement. A friend once shared his philosophy in the matter as, "Don't sweat the small stuff," then added, "and, everything is small stuff." The following is about small stuff.

Check and Checkmate

I wrote a cheek the other day
I do not know to whom
I've searched my mind
Wracked my brain
Examined every room

The note remains elusive
The bank has not a clue
My checkbook
Will not balance
I've a pile of bills past due

Why did I not make note of it
The date ... the size ... the sum?
The details still elude me
My brain has gone
Quite numb

I sat me down to meditate
To clear my mind and free
That now forgotten action
From my foggy
Memory

My frustration keeps on rising
The issue now grown large
On the balance I am counting
To avoid a new bank charge

It has grown to fifteen bucks
An exorbitant sum you'll agree
The system needs revising
My savings just net three

Three percent for all I save
Twenty for all I borrow
None of that helps me find
My check! Hell —

I'll think about it tomorrow

Pity the Poor Bureaucrat

The only thing that saves us from the bureaucracy is inefficiency. An efficient bureaucracy is the greatest threat to liberty.

Eugene McCarthy

The title is offered tongue-in-cheek, for it is always better, far better in every possible instance, to avoid the bureaucrat. When it's impossible to do so you might appreciate that your encounter is with a different species. They appear to be just like you and me, but don't be fooled. In place of a mind they have a surgically implanted manual.

It's not their fault, it is part of the job requirement, and you can meet them at any level of government. You might want to assume a blank look, feign a little ignorance, which might not be too hard for some of us. But above all, keep a sense of humor handy.

Whatever you do, do not poke them in the eye with a sharp stick. As therapy, I wrote —

Dear Medicare

I sent a letter off to you
Dispatched it weeks ago
Patiently I watch the mails
For your reply — but no
I get no answer from you
Though my need was small
Just to know what you will pay
For a simple doctor's call

A common cold was what I had
Nothing more severe
Long since, I have recovered
And now I wait to hear
What you will pay old Doc Eli
Cough syrup I bought myself
I wait in vain for your reply
My request placed on the shelf

Now, I'm not mad, or even surprised
I know your life is tough
You're busy, Oh, so busy
And money — there's never enough
You try your best from nine to eleven
And then from two to four
How much do people expect of you?
Who could ask for more?

But when you come across my note
In the file you call "dead"
Retrieve it! Resurrect it! Dust it off!
And answer it — instead

Of simply letting it lay there
Neglected and forlorn
And I might suggest you hurry a bit
Before Gabriel blows his horn

Of Cabbages and Kings

Once there lived a cabbage
In a kingdom far away
Who dreamt of fame and fortune
Among the strong who play

The world's great power games
Of wealth and war and strife
He dreamed, "If I just had a chance
I'd build a better life

A life of wealth and leisure
No wish left unfilled
I'd work real hard to have it all
Soon become quite skilled

In business lots of money I'd make
In social scenes sublime
I'd cultivate the finest friends
And use them all to climb

The ladder of success and fame
Then for office I would run
For pomp and pride and politics
Would be a lot of fun

It only takes a positive thought
An affirmation or two
For all the things we wish for
To come to me and you

While cabbage dreamed of power and fame
He heard a footstep nigh
A hand reached down and plucked him up
A hand from out the sky —

He heard a voice say, "This one's fine —
I think the best of the lot"
Cabbage was thrilled and puffed with pride
I'm the chosen one he thought

As they carried him
Into the kitchen
And dropped him
In the pot!

The Trysting Place

Meet me under the spreading yew
To find the things that we might do
In a secret place that's hid from view
Just you and me, and me and you

Delights to fill your mind with glee
We'll share there under that tiny tree
As from this crazy world we flee
Just me and you, and you and me

So come with me my playful one
Come into the shade, out of the Sun
Here in the cool of the spreading yew
You will lie with me, and I with you

VI
Writing —
Agony and Ecstasy

Agony and ecstasy serve well enough as a colorful subtitle, using polar opposites for effect, but is not accurate in describing that activity which fulfills my soul's deep desire. That is more closely echoed in the following words.

Man is not free to refuse to do the thing which gives him more pleasure than any other conceivable action.

Stendahl

A Writer's Dream

My journals are filled with the content and context of dreams. Some stand out as being more significant than others. I'm not sure that's true, but some seem to more closely relate to what is going on in the waking life.

I am sitting in a bathroom in an open barracks-like area. To my left, stretched out on his back, is a young man with long curly hair. There is another male presence lying in a upper bunk to my right.

There is no paper available for me to cleanse myself. I ask the young man lying on the floor to rise and get me some paper. He is unresponsive. I cajole, even threaten him, to no avail. Then, at last, he sits up. To encourage his response, I say, "Good! Good!" It seems to work, for he slowly, somewhat reluctantly, rises to his feet. I am encouraged now, and shout, "Excellent!" He promptly lay back down on the floor.

Frustrated, I stand up, pull up my shorts, and proceed to locate a bathroom with some paper. As I am leaving, the guy in the upper bunk observed what I have left and said, "This is bad! This is really bad!" In response I shout, "Flush it!"

Just off the barracks room I find another bathroom, small and cramped. The light does not work, and there is a strange buzzing noise coming from the ceiling, as though from an electrical malfunction. I am trying to decide whether to leave the door open since there is no light, or to close it for privacy. That was a strange concern in view of where I had just relieved myself. I think I finally closed it, but I am not sure.

I probed the dream for its meaning, while keeping in mind that all the characters, places and objects, in the drama reflect some part of my consciousness — my psyche. The drama itself is an essential element in understanding any dream, a metaphor that the unconscious mind brings to one's attention for consideration. Here is the result of my interpretation of the dream.

The dream presented a drama that characterized my perennial inner conflict concerning writing, with a bowel movement being symbolic of having produced something, a creation from the depths of my being. The drama tells me that there is no paper on which to record my efforts, and no one is willing to help.

The young man resting on the floor is the "Artist," with whom I am well acquainted. He appears to respond to the moment and need, but the effort is just too much. After all there is no paper. What is he expected to do about that? He is content to rest there and dream of what he might write.

He in the upper bunk is the "Critic," and I know him all too well. His comment, *"This is bad! This is really bad!"* is typical, as is my angry response, *"Flush it!"* Don't bother with reviewing or rewriting the result of your effort, just listen to the Critic, and scrap it. There is some perverse reward in accepting his opinion, which often echoes one lodged deep within, for it allows one to avoid further work and effort.

The heartening aspect of the drama tells me that I am actively looking for a solution to my problem, when just off the barracks room I find another space. I need that space to separate me, the Writer, from both the lazy "Artist," and the carping "Critic."

It is small, and cramped, and without light which makes it necessary for me to leave the door ajar for all to see the messy activity the creative process requires and — to see what it is that I have produced. Small, dark and cramped, it is not unlike the womb, the ultimate symbol of the creative process.

With an elegant use of symbol and metaphor my dream had portrayed the essence of my problem as well as the solution.

A look at my journals makes it painfully clear that I had spent an inordinate amount of time writing about why I was not writing. Isn't that a kick?

Writer's Cramp

The desire to write, to create with word and image, is often present while the inspiration of the muse remains elusive. It has been said that the creative act is ten percent inspiration and ninety percent perspiration. The truth of the percentages may be questioned but, it is clear that inspiration without perspiration is likely to leave one empty-handed. However, even when the two are joined one needs to know that the result may fall far short of one's expectations.

Pen in hand
I dream, hope
Wish, wait
A thick membrane
Of fog fills my skull
I await the muse
Ah! I feel movement
Something stirs
In the depths
It swells
Filled with promise
It emerges —

A bloated cliche

Agony, as in "Agony and Ecstasy," is too powerful an expression, too extreme for my taste, to describe the simple frustration of sitting with pen in hand waiting for the brain to start firing. That is not to say that it is easy to return again and again to that appointment with the self in pursuit of the muse. So what is it that impels the writer to that daily rendezvous?

Hope Eternal

Half-filled cup
Coffee grown cold
Inspiration tepid
Pen poised
Expectantly
Hope eternal
Fills the breast
What agony
What ecstasy

Uninvited

Like morning clouds and fog
It arrives on cat's paws
In the hours of darkness
And lays a shroud
Upon my heart —
Self doubt.

Broken promises to myself
Dreams denied — ignored
Disbelieved —
Form brooding clouds
On the mountain peaks of
My aspirations

Clouds scatter
In the morning Sun
My Soul rejoices
In the Light of —
Self-Love

Driven

Write! Right?
Do it! Don't think!
A swarm of
Half-formed dreams
And desires —

There is no peace.
Its claws sunk
Deep in my gut
Poetry? Prose?
Essay? Article?

Muse or monster
Whatever —
Don't give a damn.
Grab that pen and
Move it — Move it!

Make those marks.
Ah! Peace!

Mute Muse

With pen in hand I await the muse
That tantalizing creature
I'll write the great American tale
Or perhaps a Sunday feature
Critics all will think it great
As they carefully peruse
The gems my pen will generate
To entertain, delight, amuse
Nothing happens, my mind a blank
My pen remains inert
I cannot think of a single thing
My brain begins to hurt
The empty page stares back at me
With quiet contempt it seems
While I, as empty as the page, have
No clever plots, no themes
My mind is stuck in emptiness
No matter how I yen
So it shouldn't be a total loss
I'll sit and practice Zen

Worlds and Whirls

There are worlds and whirls
And both are real
Yet both are make-believe
It appears the worlds
Consist of whirls
Our senses so perceive
From this perception
There's born each day
A multitude of thought
Of love and joy —
Or fear and doubt —
While truth is what we sought
Round and round
They flit and fly
While in their wake
They leave —
Worlds and whirls
Each, Oh, so real —

And all — so make-believe

Pens 'n Stuff

Books 'n glasses 'n pens 'n stuff
My usual array
Things I need to ply my trade
For yet another day

Pens I need to make the marks
My glasses just to see
Books are my companions
Writ by others just like me

The stuff's my own I must admit
Its value can't be vouched for
But the books 'n glasses n' pens
I need, in order to create more

Shifting Moments

A different pen
Another voice
Distinctive
In its essence

As I am different
Day to day
In feeling, choice
And presence

I bless the change
Life brings to pass
In every
Obsolescence

Destiny

Empty white page—
Inviting, challenging
Seductive
Beckons, nay
Demands
The pen's caress
Ah! For this
I was born—
To receive, record
Reveal
The movement
Of Mind

Thirty spokes converge at one hub;
What is not there makes the wheel useful.
Clay is shaped to form a vessel;
What is not there makes the vessel useful.
Doors and windows are cut to form a room;
What is not there makes the room useful.
Therefore, take advantage of what is there,
By making use of what is not.
                              Tao Te Ching (11)

The empty white page and — this day.

VII
Work —
Love made Visible

The subtitle is from The Prophet, by Kahlil Gibran, who wrote, "You work that you may keep pace with the earth and the soul of the earth ... And when you work 'with love you bind yourself to yourself, and to one another, and to God."

Serendipity

Serendipity is described as an unexpected joy-filled happening, like a gift you did not anticipate, or a letter from someone you intended to write but whose address you have lost. It can be a totally surprising result that arises out of some piece of work — or play — where you have one purpose in mind and find it has blessed you in ways you never envisioned.

One that I treasure happened as I worked on an assignment from an art class in watercolor. The class was called Aquamedia, a free-wheeling exploration of color and form that combined experimentation with discipline.

The task at hand was to draw a collection of basic shapes; a sphere, cone, cylinder, and box, and paint them with particular emphasis on the element of value — the interplay of light and shadow upon the objects.

I was happy with the initial drawing and decided to do a monochrome study in blue. But when I laid the first swash of color upon it I was aghast, I felt I had ruined it. I continued however and, when it was finished I felt a surprising sense of elation, of discovery. I liked it!

What started out as a routine exercise filled me with delight, a childlike wonder, at the final result. It was a lesson of value that went beyond the appreciation of light and shadow.

I found myself gazing at it in rapt joy. It was as though I had given birth, and the child was surprisingly beautiful. It prompted the following.

A Lesson of Value

Out of the formless
I appear
The shapes of your world
Played upon
By light and shadow
I beckon, entice, seduce
Your eye
Your hand
Your heart

The shapes had come alive with color and the interplay of light and shadow, and presented a valuable lesson within a lesson of value. Keep working past the doubts with patience and trust and allow the thing to reveal its own unique nature and beauty. Serendipity awaits!

My Work, My Blessing

This morning, after Linda left for work, I sat with pen in hand intending to write, feeling that I should write. Resistance took on a life of its own. I had nothing to write about, not a single worthwhile idea or impulse came to mind.

I drifted into a familiar dull lassitude, as one might feel when wrapped in a soft white cottony world — devoid of sound, or sight, or stimuli of any kind.

I did not recognize it as depression, and yet the symptoms of that malady, that dis-ease, were clearly present; feeling stuck, blocked, with no clear sense of direction.

It was ennui, a lovely sounding word that describes an aimless drifting of mind and heart, a place and time without any apparent purpose that had me in its soft, seductive clutches.

I returned to the bedroom and decided to just be with the feeling, or lack thereof. I lay quiet and relaxed, yet alert and open-minded like a curious investigator interested only in what might happen next. At first nothing, but then — I saw it clearly.

I was suffering from a chronic case of what psychologists call grandiosity. I didn't just want to write, I wanted the acclaim and fame that comes with writing a Pulitzer Prize winner, and I wanted it without any effort. No struggle, just the flash of unabashed genius making itself

155

known. Then I remembered a wonderful line attributed to W. C. Handy; *"I ain't much God, but I'm all I've got."* The words, like a splash of ice water, jarred me awake with the realization that whatever I have got, much or little, is what I have to work with.

Lying there, I felt a change take place — an epiphany. In the place of the grand visions about what my life and my work should be, a deep and abiding sense of trust and gratitude filled me. How blessed I was to have work to do, tasks waiting for my hands, my mind. Not just my work as a minister, but the ever-present tasks and duties that flow from being a husband, a householder, a friend. How fortunate!

What would my life be without all that? How empty! The lines from a poem that I first read in high school came to me.

Let me but do my work from day to day.
In field or forest, at desk or loom,
In roaring market place or tranquil room;
Let me but find it in my heart to say,
When vagrant wishes beckon me astray —
"This is my work, my blessing, not my doom;
Of all who live, I am the one by whom
This work can best be done in the right way."

Somewhere I had read or heard the phrase *a direct and simple soul,* they reminded me of the plain and powerful value and dignity of the work that fills our days.

The answer to my writing block, that which would dissipate the ennui, would be the work of a plain and direct Soul. The gift, the joy, was to be found in the doing, the writing itself. Pray God that it be directed by, and reveal the power of, a plain and simple Soul. The idea is beautifully captured in the balance of Henry Van Dyke's poem.

Then shall I see it not too great, nor small,
To suit my spirit and to prove my powers;
Then shall I cheerful greet the laboring hours.
And cheerful turn, when the long shadows fall
At eventide, to play and love and rest,
Because I know for me my work is best.
Henry Van Dyke, <u>The Outlook</u>

Minister's Migraine

I know of no Minister who has not had his or her bouts with the board of directors from time to time. Change, new programs, the desire to serve, to grow, to build — each in their own time demands the attention of the board, and of the Minister. Often the issues are deliberated and a consensus arrived at fairly easily, while at other times there is robust discourse, disagreement, and discontent, followed by the disappearance of one or more board members. One such time at our church provided inspiration for the following.

The Solution

There is a deep and
Cherished resistance
To change of any kind
When the thing that needs
The most to change
Is just a change of mind
When faced with situations
And opportunities anew
The cry most heard
Throughout the church
"That's one thing we can't do!"
"The By-Laws read
We have always done
Statistics clearly show —"
The groans and cries
All multiply
"That just isn't done — you know."
Another month flows swiftly by
Or perhaps a year or two
The situation remains unchanged
The Board's in a terrible stew
The figures look bad
Prospects are grim
The future looks most sinister
The Board confers and all agree
The solution is
Slay the minister!

Wabi Sabi

When I finally move past the excuses and put pen to paper I am immediately caught up in the process. My hand moves across the paper leaving a trail of ink marks where only moments before there was a clean, white surface. The marks left on the paper may have no specific meaning. They may be the result of doodles left in the wake of the pen's aimless movement over the surface but they are — unique and personal. They bear the stamp, the imprint, of only one individual.

In that simple act I have left something of myself on the paper, letters and lines that flowed from my brain, my gut, my hand, captured at one particular moment in time. Even if there is no serious focused intent to convey an idea or emotion, it does not matter. Like an unfolding painting it stands by itself. It needs no purpose. It IS! It makes its own statement.

The Japanese call it wabi sabi, the unique beauty and nature of a thing flawed, like a cracked and mended piece of pottery. The Chinese refer to it as the uncarved block, that which has its own flaws, imperfections, and natural beauty. It led me to ask the question — does it matter?

160

Does it Matter?

Does it matter if our work is recognized? It seems to matter a great deal. We are certainly conditioned culturally to look for it, to be motivated by it — the approval and applause of others. The need is internalized early in life, and left to its own devices can grow into a monstrous taskmaster.

The need to be thought worthy by others, when internalized becomes the Critic, the Censor, and the Perfectionist. And then, God help us when the natural urge rises within us to create, to embrace the Artist within, in the presence of this over-bearing, hyper-critical creature living within.

To be free of its stifling presence, to create with any sense of authenticity, we must ultimately find the will and courage to surrender the need for such approval from others and — from our selves. The very instant we do that we take back our power.

Lao Tzu, in the Tao Te Ching, suggests.

Produce things, cultivate things;
Produce but do not possess,
Act without expectation,
Advance without dominating,
These are called the Subtle Powers.

Tao Te Ching (10)

161

Does It Matter

Does it matter so much?
Does it matter at all
To leave our mark
For men to recall?

Marks disappear
Tales are forgot
Does it matter at all?
I rather think not

Then why this struggle
For power and fame
Pushing and pulling
A wearisome game

Jousting with windmills
Fighting with ghosts
Piling up trinkets
Who has the most?

Round like a dog
Chasing its tail
Pause for a moment
Consider the snail —

He doesn't hurry
He doesn't fret
He doesn't scamper
Or run, and

The mark he leaves
In the cool morning wet
Disappears —
In the rising sun

Marks disappear
Tales are forgot
Does it matter at all?
I rather think not

VIII
Why Me God?

I have observed that this question is always asked in times of trouble, never when things are going well. We need someone, or something, to blame for the bad times, while we eagerly accept credit for the good.

It's a foolish question, asked of a God made in man's image and likeness, who's answer might well be, "Why not you?"

A Survivors' Affair

Thomas Mann wrote, *"A man's dying is more the survivors' affair than his own."*

My first close-up look at death came ten thousand miles from home on an obscure island lost in the vastness of the Pacific — Peleliu. It is an insignificant outcropping of coral, measuring ten square miles, northeast of the Philippines, where more than fifty years ago men fought like primal beasts over its possession. In the space of ninety days the blood of more than twenty thousand dead and wounded was spilled on a few square miles of now-forgotten real estate. It was there that I saw death up close and personal, brutal and unforgettable. I was nineteen — and a proud Marine.

It was there that I first asked the question — what is it that marks one for death and another for life? It seems sometimes as though there is a gigantic crap game being played among the gods with the outcome resting on the throw of the dice from some celestial hand, and we ask — "Why?" We feel that it has to somehow make sense. It doesn't! But the question, like a recurring bad dream, haunts the mind of anyone who has ever been in combat — and survived. "How is it that I lived and my buddies died?"

I was in the third wave of the assault, with a full pack on my back and a seventy pound radio, the size of a microwave oven, strapped to my chest. We stood grouped in the belly of an amphibious tractor as it plowed its torturous way over the reefs toward shore, while we saw others like it blown out of the water by Japanese artillery firing from the ridges. It reminded me of the line of little white ducks that creep across the back of a carnival shooting gallery. We were *sitting ducks!*

It seems we were lucky, we missed being blown out of the water, and the beast that carried us in its belly finally shuddered to a stop a few yards short of the beach. It opened its mouth as the landing ramp was lowered and disgorged us into surf up to our waist.

I struggled against the sucking drag of the wet sand and water and finally made it to the beach — a bloody brutal beach already littered with the bodies of comrades.

Someone shouted, *"Get down you dumb bastard, they're right there!"* And I really hit the beach. The blistering sand, the cries of wounded, the constant artillery and small arms fire all fused together to create a living hell on earth. The blood-red scorching sun finally surrendered to the Pacific and darkness descended on the first day.

By nightfall we had gained a few hundred yards and our initial objective, a small airstrip. We hunkered down. Exhausted, I scraped a shallow foxhole in the sand, and waited and watched. The darkness was shattered by the intermittent flash and blast of incoming artillery rounds, and the return fire from our ships off shore. The ground trembled under the pounding — and I with it.

It was there that I first looked death, the distinct possibility of my death, right in the face. It's true that the Marines turn boys into men, but nothing in the training can prepare anyone for that moment, for the crystal-clear realization — I could die here. At any moment, I could die.

By morning of the second day a great deadening calm came over me when I decided I was either going to live, or I was going to die, and I didn't have a whole lot to say about which was to happen. In that moment my mind, my very soul, was etched deeply in some irrevocable way. A cold shield settled around my heart.

In the days that followed, I went about my duties shielded by that coldness, cloaked in it — a stone where my heart had been. There was no sense of worry about living or dying, each day had its duties and one day followed another — and another. On the surface there was no change but, deep within the warrior was born — I survived.

Years later, while attending a class on Death and Dying in Contemporary Society, I wrote a poem in which the memories of Peleliu combined with the thoughtless act of a young boy. I had killed a bird with a stone from my slingshot. It fell from the power line — dead. I picked it up and held its tiny feathery body in my hand. Ashamed of what I had done, and overwhelmed by a deep sadness, I stood in the middle of the road — and wept. The awful finality of what I had done seared my soul. The combined memories inspired.

Stolen Gift

Quiet country lane
Swallows perched
On a power line
Boy with a slingshot
A stone flies
A bird dies
A boy cries
Mangled beach —
Peleliu
Lying in the sand —
Half a man
HELP ME! Help me —
I'm a—li---ve
The sand is red
Where he has bled
And he —
Is dead!

Blessed in countless ways by what the Psalmist called a goodly heritage I have never experienced the misery, hopelessness, and indignity that is the daily fare of the homeless. As a result, God help me, I was arrogant in my ignorance whenever I saw an apparently healthy individual begging for a handout. The following imaginary dialogue was the result.

Why Me, God?

Man - Why me God? Why me?
GOD - WHY NOT YOU?

That, if you'll pardon my saying so, is one Hell of a response. I thought you were a God of love.
I AM. I LOVE YOU.

Tell me another one. Since you are All-knowing, Then you know that I've tried to live a good life.
TRUE.

Well, what has it gotten me? I lie among strangers, wrapped in newspapers to keep from freezing. Like a stray dog I exist on scraps from another's table. If I had the guts, I'd end it!
YES, YOU WOULD.

What? I thought suicide was a sin?
IT IS.

Can you speak in more than two or three words?
YES.

Screw you! I get more sense talking to a bum.
THE TRUTH IS THAT YOU DO, TO USE YOUR
QUAINT EXPRESSION, "SCREW ME" WHEN
YOU PERSIST IN SCREWING YOURSELF. YOU
HAVE LIFE, AN ABLE BODY, A MIND TO ASK
QUESTIONS LIKE THESE YOU ALSO HAVE THE
GUTS TO END IT. I HAVE NOT ABANDONED
YOU. YOU HAVE ABANDONED YOU. GO FIND
A MIRROR. LOOK CLOSELY AND ASK, "WHY
ME GOD?" THEN LISTEN — REALLY LISTEN
TO THE ANSWER.

I LOVE YOU. I AM WITH YOU ALWAYS!

I wrote the above imagined dialogue more
out of ignorance than insight. I have since
learned that more than a third, perhaps as
many as half of the homeless is afflicted with
some form of mental illness. They have been
literally dumped on the street, while mental
hospitals close their doors. Some towns and
cities have found a solution that prompted me to
write the following short, short story.

Greyhound Therapy

The screech of airbrakes pierced the night and mixed with the phantoms in his mind. Like a swimmer struggling up from the depths, he awakes with a gasp and lurches upright in the seat. The side of his face is numb with cold where it had rested against the window of the bus. He rubbed the fog of his breath off the glass and peered out the window.

No one sat near him on the trip, and everyone has now gotten off the bus. He felt under his seat for his bundle, slipped his hand under the rope tie and, grabbing the back of the seat in front of him, rose to his feet and shuffled to the exit door.

A blast of frigid air staggered him as he stepped from the bus and collided with a woman waiting to get on. Strands of gray hair peak from under her hat, which sits squarely over a no-nonsense face. She reminds him of someone, but he can't remember who. He mumbled an apology, as the woman recoiled from his touch, fear and disgust written on her face. She folded her arms protectively around her handbag, and stepped around him to board the bus.

Through rheumy bloodshot eyes he followed her movements, while he tried to remember who she reminded him of. He shook his head, like an old prize-fighter, to clear it.

173

It was hard for him to remember things. Turning away, he picked up his bundle and moved toward the entrance to the terminal. The lighted sign over the entrance read, "Cleveland." He wonders what the hell he is doing in Cleveland. He doesn't remember buying a ticket, but then he doesn't remember where he was yesterday.

He looped the rope tie of his bundle over his shoulder and made his way into the station. He must have been on the bus for a long time, he thinks, as he looks for a men's room. He sees the sign, enters and steps up to a vacant urinal.

Standing next to him is a guy in a three-piece suit who manages to look everywhere but at him. He's used to that, it's like he's invisible.

His fingers work their way past the flapping wings of the olive-drab overcoat he found in a trash bin in Columbus. Columbus! He remembers! That's where he was last night, in jail in Columbus. Remembering makes him feel better.

A shiver rippled through his bony frame. Beneath the overcoat he wore a thread-bare flannel shirt, and a baggy pair of trousers tied at the waist with a piece of the same rope that secures his bundle.

In the waiting room he found an empty bench, and sat on the end. His bundle next to him, his empty pale eyes dart furtively from face to face. The faces turn away, avoiding the sight of a smelly pile of cast-off clothes with the remnants of a man inside. He picked up his bundle and cradled it in his lap. He learned a long time ago, soon after he was released from the hospital, that you have to hang onto your bundle.

He's hungry, always hungry it seems, and he needs to find a place to flop for the night, and maybe a bowl of hot soup. Out of the corner of his eye he sees a couple of uniforms shoulder their way in from the cold. He looks down and bends to tighten the knots on the bundle. He hates cops, they make him afraid.

Slowly, reluctantly, he looks at two sets of shiny black shoes next to his bundle. The end of ebony nightstick poked at it, accompanied by a voice — "What have you got in there?"
"Nothin'."

"Nothing?" The voice, colder than the weather outside, now has a brittle edge that sends ripples of fear coursing along his nerve endings.
"Just some things ... and ... medicine," he says, barely above a whisper.

"What kind of medicine ... Drugs?
"No he mutters." He doesn't look up. Maybe if he doesn't look up they will just go away. Leave him alone.

The cops don't move.

"It's to quiet the voices," he says. "The doctor said I should take it every day, only sometimes ... I forget."

"Did you just come in on a bus?"
"Yeah."

"Where'd you come from?"
"Columbus ... I think. Yeah. Columbus."

"What are you doing in Cleveland?"
"I dunno."

\

"Why did you leave Columbus?"
"I dunno."

"Well you can't hang around here. There's a shelter over on Fifteenth. Get out of here. Move on!"

He snatched up his bundle, and stumbled out into the night. He knew without looking that the cops are standing there, watching him. In the pocket of his overcoat, the pocket that doesn't have a hole in it, he fingers two crumpled one dollar bills.

He could get a bunk for the night for a buck, he thinks, and still have something left over for coffee, or a drink, in the morning. A drink! He shudders. God, he could sure use a drink.

It started to rain, rain mixed with snow, carried on the knife-edge of a wind off the lakes. Christ, it's cold! He pulls the navy skull cap down over his ears. Did he take his medicine today? He can't remember. He could remember better if the voices would only stop.

Blinking neon lights splash the wet sidewalk with pulsating color; red, green, red, green. Then he's inside, and he lays the two crumpled bills on the counter. "Gimme a bottle of Thunderbird," he mutters.

Hugging the bottle, he moved off down the street into the darkness, and the cold, pausing from time to time to take a long pull at the bottle nestled in the brown paper bag. He knows they're not going to let him in the shelter if he's been drinking.

What the hell, he doesn't know where the shelter is anyway. He stepped out of the rain and wind into the partial shelter of a doorway to a closed shop. He drops his bundle on the ground, sits on it, and leans his back against closed door. Tugging the coat more tightly around him, he drinks the rest of the Thunderbird. It warms him and ... it quiets the voices.

It was nearly dawn when the cops found him, huddled in the doorway of the shop, his stiffened arms wrapped around his bundle. The rain had turned to snow during the night and the temperature had plunged. The cops called it in,

177

"This is unit 452, we got a stiff in the doorway at 113 South Street. Do the suits want to roll on it?"

There is a pause followed by the voice of the dispatcher, "Any sign of violence?"

"No," they reply, "just another homeless drifter who ran out of Thunderbird."

The Dispatcher advised them that the detectives are not interested, but that he will notify the Coroner to have the body picked up, while they go to the morgue to determine the drifter's identity, so next of kin can be notified.
At the morgue the officers find no trace of identification on the body. They loosen the frozen knots and open the bundle the guy carried. Wrapped in a torn Army poncho they find an old gym bag containing a worn pair of jeans, a flannel shirt, two pairs of socks, a pair of underwear, a Bic razor, a comb with teeth missing, a pen-knife with a broken blade, and a old faded photograph of the derelict when he was a young man.

The man in the photo had a slack-jawed look on his face, and his arm around a tired looking older gray-haired woman in a print dress. On the back of the photo, written in pencil, was scrawled, *"Mom and Joey, 1969."*

Also in the gym bag, the officers found a medicine bottle that contained five tablets. The faded label read: "Centerville State Hospital, Centerville, Ohio. Joseph X. Kelly. Risperidone 40 mg. One tablet three times daily." As he tossed the bottle back in the bundle, the cop growled — "He shouldn't have been on the street, they're still doing it."

"What's that?" his partner asked.

"More than a third of the street people are mentally ill," he replied. Joe Citizen wants them off the street, and out of sight, and jail is not an answer. Most cities don't have the resources to provide the care they need, so they found a solution. They buy the poor bastards a ticket and put them on a bus to ... anywhere else. They call it Greyhound Therapy."

The End

IX
A Goodly Heritage

"The Lord is my chosen portion and my cup; thou holdest my lot.

The lines have fallen for me in pleasant places; yea, I have a goodly heritage." Psalm 16.5-6

Grandma's Kitchen

When I awoke this morning the image my Grandma filled my senses in that uncharted land that lies between sleeping and waking. I embraced the moment and for a time I was once again a little boy enveloped in the warmth and love of Grandma's kitchen. It struck me for the first time just how tiny was the kitchen of that old farmhouse. Not then, of course. Then it was the center of much of my world, a small world to be sure, but a safe one. The whole world seemed safe — then.

I find it fascinating now, but not surprising, that the images of Grandma's kitchen are borne in memory by the smells of the place. The tantalizing aroma of salt-port sizzling in the pan, along with frying potatoes and onions can in an instant carry me back to that common, ordinary, magical place— Grandma's kitchen.

It was filled to the brim with the fragrance and feel of home and family, food and, wood smoke when the stove was not drawing right, or a gust of wind created a downdraft. Spices and fruit added their heady presence, and just off this tiny universe there was a pantry with even more wonders for the nose and eyes, and sometimes the hands, of a curious little boy.

There was a small couch set against the wall just inside the door, covered with spreads of cotton, a heavy woolen "horse" blanket and pillows covered with embroidery. That old couch seemed to retain something of the essence of every person who had rested there. It seemed, whenever I lay down on it, to reach out and embrace me like an old friend.

Two things dominated Grandma's kitchen; one was the kitchen table covered in oilcloth, with tiny lines and cracks where it reluctantly formed to the shape of the table's corners. The other, which seemed to fill half the kitchen, was a huge, wood-burning stove. The lids to the firebox had to be lifted by using a small hand tool. Lift one of those lids and, summer or winter, you would find a fire burning, cherry-red.

That stove, and Grandma's magic, brought forth a steady stream of love and nourishment; fresh-baked bread, roasts and stews, and — pies. From that oven there was born pies — apple, pumpkin, peach, blueberry, strawberry and rhubarb so incredible that they had to be touched by the hand of God herself — as indeed they were.

How blessed I was by the large measures of love and strength that poured into my life from that place. How is it that it has taken me so long to fully appreciate the precious gifts that flowed so freely from — Grandma's kitchen?

Giving and Receiving

How difficult it seems to be for us to learn the power of giving, and the inseparable link that exists between giving and receiving. We have heard the *Law of Increase* stated in many ways, from many wise sources, but none with greater clarity and wisdom than this.

Give and it will be given to you; good measure, pressed down, shaken together, running over, will be put in your lap. For the measure you give will be the measure you get back. Luke 6.37

Caught up in a world of appearances of lack and limitation, where scarcity is the law, we are likely to be convinced that we must first get before we can give. That the opposite is true is a lesson that is difficult for many to accept.

The lesson that you must first give in order to receive is one I learned from my grandfather when I was just a little boy, but it took me years to really understand and accept it. He called it priming the pump, and the encounter went something like this.

"How do you get the water, Grandfather?" Sonny asked, as he pumped the handle in vain. He watched intently as his Grandfather poured water in the top of the old pump.

"Now pump the handle, boy." He said. I did, and sweet, cold, clear water bubbled forth from the spout.

"It's like life," Grandfather said. 'You've got to put some in before you get any out." Thinking about it years later inspired:

Priming the Pump

You have to put some in you know
Before you get some out
A little water in the top
Returns more from the spout
A little effort first applied
To any dream or plan
It's what's required —
It's the Law
For nature or for man
The seed must first be planted
The ore must first be mined
The lesson is we first must give
To reap things after their kind
Love begets love in abundant flow
The measure you give is the seed
But you have to put some in, you know
To receive all the things you need

Grandma Ross' Legacy

At an early age she had to leave school to take care of several younger brothers and sisters, due to a death in the family. It has been said that what doesn't kill you makes you stronger. Helen Ross grew strong, and remained that way until her death at the age of 96.

When Helen's brothers and sisters no longer needed her, she was there for countless others throughout her long life. One of them was my wife, Linda, who inherited from Grandma Ross an indomitable spirit and a loving caring heart. One could not ask for a richer legacy.

Two simple poems hung framed in Grandma Ross' kitchen for many years that reflect a warm spirit, a gracious heart and a lively sense of humor.

Kitchen Prayer

Lord of all pots and pans and things
Since I've not time to be
A saint by doing lovely things
Or watching late with Thee
Or dreaming in the dawn light
Or storming Heaven's gates
Make me a saint by getting meals
And washing up the plates
Although I must have Martha's hands

I have a Mary mind
And when I black the boots and shoes
Thy sandals Lord I find
I think of how they trod the earth
What time I scrub the floor
Accept this meditation Lord
I have not time for more
Warm the kitchen with Thy Love
And Light it with Thy peace
Forgive me all my worrying
And make my grumbling cease
Thou who didst love to give men food
In room or by the sea
Accept this service that I do
I do it unto Thee.

Klara Mundres

A poet once this
Sentence penned:
"The one is rich who
Has a friend!"
I read it and I
Thought: How true!
He must have had
A friend like —
You!

Author unknown

These homely powerful expressions of love
are each contained in an inexpensive frame, with
glass on the front and paper covering the back.
The paper, now turned brown and fragile,

speaks of their age. On the back of each is written in Grandma Ross' careful script, "Gift from Marty Haines."

These things were among a few personal effects my wife, Linda, received from her beloved grandmother. Something of the spirit of Grandma Ross had, like precious oil, left its indelible imprint on these simple cherished things.

Such gifts are made sacred by the love and care of an extraordinary human being. Like autographed copies of a rare original they radiate an aura of love straight from the hands and great heart of an uncommon and unique woman — Grandma Helen Ross.

X
Retirement?!

*It seems like such a lovely idea —
when you are young. But like all things in
life it has two sides, a truth that awaits all
who live long enough, and one I came to
learn firsthand.*

Retire? Never!

To retire from a lifetime of work seems like such an alluring prospect, particularly to the young. We had a tongue-in-cheek saying when I was a young man, living in New Jersey; "It's the law! When you get to be 65 you have to retire and move to Florida."

It seems that my life had hardly begun when suddenly I was 63, and living in Columbus, Ohio. Linda and I owned a security services company that employed over 300 people, and for nearly four years we also ministered to a thriving church with a growing congregation, but all that was about to change.

I suppose we could mark it down to the alignment of the planets. It was 1987, the year of the Harmonic Convergence, and the air was filled with the voices of those who were predicting the end of the world. In a sense our world, as we knew it, was about to come to an end.

We had spent the weekend of the Convergence at Serpent's Mound, a National Park, established on the site of an Indian burial ground in the shape of a serpent, in southern Ohio. We were sharing our motorhome with another couple from the church.

It was sunset, and we sat together talking quietly over a glass of wine, completely caught up in the hushed joy of the moment. I felt that I was just making a passing comment when I said, "I would like to do this full time." Our friend Bob's quick reply was, "Why don't you?" Bob is an out-of-the-box thinker, one of the many reasons I like him.

I didn't answer then, but the question hung in the air and in my mind. It became clear that it was in Linda's mind as well, for we had recently wondered whether we owned the company, or it owned us.

On the return trip to Columbus, we answered both questions. At the church board meeting that evening I gave sixty days notice, and the following morning put the company assets up for sale, along with the building that housed it. That was followed by a "For Sale" on the front lawn of our home.

In the space of two months we sold everything and ventured forth. And it was wonderful! For nearly a year we traveled the country, spending much of the time in the southwest. Major decisions of the day included, when to go to the pool, and where to travel next.

It was wonderful and we piled up a store of luscious memories but ultimately within the fullness there was a subtle sense of something missing. That feeling is echoed in the following selection.

Morning in the Campground

Awake to the cry of gulls
The morning sun
Astride the back
Of an ocean breeze
In my nose and mouth
The sweet taste of love
Strong, black coffee
The day stretches out
The hours easy
Full, yet empty
In my guts
An echo of unrest
Where was the need?
To be up — engaged?
My gladiator's heart
Misses the arena!
Sometimes
In the warm lazy Sun
Of morning
In the campground

It's Not Over 'Til it's Over

The idea of retiring, as I envisioned it and as I have observed others at that stage of life, has never held any great attraction for me. To be unoccupied, unengaged in mind and heart in some purposeful activity that challenges me is more of a nightmare than a dream. Unoccupied, the word reminds me of like an empty house and that is no place to live.

For one who has retired from a job or profession into which they have poured their life, the idea of beginning something new can be strange, even frightening. But I believe with all my heart that that is brightest, healthiest thing they can do.

Failing that there is likely to be a feeling of emptiness and the growing conviction that it's all over, that life — vibrant, enthusiastic, engaged life — is now over. The truth is that it is not over. If you're still here, God has work for you to do.

These thoughts prompted the following.

Begin Again?!

Begin again! I ask, for what?
My back is sore, my eyes are shot
Spend too much time upon the pot
Begin again? I rather think not.

It's never too late is your reply?
Make a difference, reach for the sky
Make your mark, do your thing
Now's the time for a new beginning

, *Begin again! Don't count the cost*
Don't think of the times you have lost
Remember the days when you have won
The prize you sought, the good fight fought

You're still here you've got things to do
Deeds in this life, that only you
With that special talent can fulfill
But sitting there you never will

You're retired you say
What does that mean?
Have you just quit living?
Is hat your scene?

How old will you be
If you don't do a thing
But sit there —
Sadly wondering

What you might have done
Had you simply tried
To fulfill those dreams
That you feel have died?

Get off your butt
And into the game
Take the dare —
Risk the pain

The prize can be yours
To have and to share
But you'll never get it
Just sitting there

Begin again!

It's Never Too Late

He traded a golf bag for a book bag and launched a new career.

A quiet suspense hung in the air, broken by the scrape of a chair, a nervous cough, or the rustle of shuffled papers, as the minute hand of the clock on the wall click-clicked its way toward the hour. Late arrivals slipped quietly into the room, faces closed, self-absorbed. I sat in the front row, feeling vulnerable, exposed to the curious eyes of those behind me. I would be sixty-five in November and this was my first day back in a college classroom.

The class was on Creative Writing, and I was curious to see how committing to the discipline of a college class would give form and substance to a life-long desire to write creatively—effectively. I did not realize that it would mark the beginning of a new career.

I discovered that day that John Dewey was absolutely right when he said, "Education is not preparation for life, it is life itself." I had no idea then just how prophetic those words would be to my future, and the fulfillment of a dream that lay buried in my youth.

I also found that I was not alone. A growing number of "seasoned" citizens, not satisfied with the empty round of time-filling activities that often come with retirement, arehitting the books in classrooms of colleges and universities everywhere.

Exploding the myth that you can't teach an old dog a new trick, they are finding the classroom to be an open door to a new lease on life. Engaged in what has become known as "life-long learning" they are creating new careers, earning degrees, or simply rediscovering the sheer joy of learning. Research into life-long learning has shown that there is no limit to learning imposed by age alone.

On the contrary, a study done at Pennsylvania State University in 1986, where the participants ranged in age from 64 to 95, revealed that it is the amount of mental stimulation a person receives, rather than age that determines mental ability. Further, that even when mental functioning declines over the years, it starts improving with new learning.

It seems that age, like beauty, is more in the eye of the beholder. When my wife Linda told her 95 year old grandmother that she had returned to college to earn a degree, Grandma's response was, "You're too damned old to be going to school. Why, you'll be over 50 by the time you graduate."

Undaunted, Linda replied, "Grandma, how old will I be if I don't do it?"

That is not to say that the step does not take a certain kind of courage, it does. The older student might not hear as well as they used to or see quite as clearly, and there many like Linda who work full-time while doing it.

The older person who has reentered the classroom may contend with these issues, while the youngster is likely to be struggling toward some sense of identity and purpose. I found that these differences quickly disappear in the mutual effort to absorb the material and respond to the demands of the classroom. I can still recall the pleasure I felt when a youngster asked me if I would make a copy of my notes for a class he was going to miss.

The teachers and professors proved to be just as welcoming. "Returning older students are some of our best students," the head of the Arts department once said to me. "They are here because they want to be; they are highly motivated and focused. It is not uncommon," he added, "to find them preparing for a new career." And though I did not realize it when I took that first class that is exactly what happened to me.

As a young man I had dreamed of being a writer. Then there was WWII and the Marines, followed by a marriage and a career in law enforcement, followed by one in business, and finally, another in the ministry. A lot of living happened between that dream and my return to the classroom, but I was to realize my dream at last.

In July of last year I published my first book, and am well into producing a second. I am doing what I love and loving what I do. But none of it would have happened had I not sat with others in that classroom more than a decade ago, waiting to begin yet again.

Emerson wrote, *"Life only avails, not the having lived,"* and in the same essay, *"Power ceases in the instant of repose; it resides in the moment of transition from a past to a new state."*

If your life has become one of too much repose and not enough power, if you think you are too old—think again. Seize the moment, reclaim your power. Whether you want to learn an exotic language, earn a degree, launch a new career, or simply fill your days with new interests and ideas, there is a classroom waiting somewhere for you.

About the Author

Edward V. Tuttle, D.D., now devotes full-time to counseling, writing, and lecturing. His most recent work <u>Sacred Stories Sacred Dreams; Bible Myth and Metaphor</u> (Pathways of Lights 2002) is currently in book stores and on-line. He lives in Santa Maria, California.

References

1.   Wing, R. L. (1986) *The Tao of Power,* New York; Dolphin Book Doubleday.

2.   Emerson, Ralph Waldo, *Essays and Journals,* (1968) International Collectors Library, Nelson Doubleday, Inc.